OLSEN   1, 50

MARK LEONARD is Director of Foreign Policy at the Centre for European Reform where he works on transatlantic relations, the Middle East and EU–China relations. Previously he was Director of the Foreign Policy Centre, a think-tank he founded at the age of 24; a 'Transatlantic Fellow' at the German Marshall Fund in Washington DC; and a researcher at the think-tank Demos. Mark has established a reputation as one of the liveliest thinkers on global issues through his regular commentary in many of the world's leading newspapers and journals, and his consultancy work with governments and business. He lives in Camden Town.

WWW.MARKLEONARD.NET

why europe will run the 21st century

MARK LEONARD

PUBLICAFFAIRS
New York

Library of Congress Cataloging-in-Publication Data
Leonard, Mark, 1974–
Why Europe will run the 21st century / Mark Leonard.—1st ed.
    p. cm.
Includes index.
ISBN-10: 1-58648-364-1
ISBN-13: 978-1-58648-364-7
1. Balance of power—Forecasting. 2. Europe—Foreign relations—21st
century—Forecasting. 3. World politics—21st century—Forecasting. 4.
International relations—Forecasting. I. Title: Why Europe will run the 21st
century. II. Title.
JZ1313.L46   2005
327.1'12'0905—dc22
                    2005048874

First Edition

10 9 8 7 6 5 4 3 2 1

For Dick, Irène, Miriam and Gabrielle

CONTENTS

PREFACE

Why Europe

This is not a book about the merits of Brie over Velveeta, of the architectural Baroque over corporate post-modernism, or of the thirty-five hour working week over America's "long hours" culture. Nor is it a loose claim on behalf of Europe's culture or lifestyle being in some way preferable to others around the world. It is about power. It looks at the source and application of power in a number of fields, and assumes that power is not merely the show of force but the ability to shape the world and pull potentially hostile blocs into a collaborative orbit based on a shared set of values.

The book attempts to show that what began as a modest trading union in two commodities essential to post–World War 2 reconstruction – coal and steel – has become in part by design and part by accident a community that, despite its public disputes, is poised to be the dominant global influence of the 21st Century, both through its own actions and as a model to the rest of the world.

The creation of the European Union arguably owes more to America than any other nation. To argue the case for Europe, and a strong Europe at that, is not an anti-American position: it's to acknowledge America's role in the foundation of the EU. I am a passionate, and grateful, Atlanticist who supported humanitarian interventions in Bosnia, Kosovo, and could have supported an Iraq war under different circumstances. As much as I believe in international law and the United Nations, I also believe that we cannot hide behind these institutions to justify inaction, whether in the face of genocide in Rwanda or Darfur, or of weapons of mass destruction in the hands of terrorists.

The European Union is in many ways an American creation. Without the Marshall Plan, the American nuclear umbrella, and the help of Uncle Sam when things went wrong, it would never have happened. But today, for the first time in 50 years, it is the US that needs Europe's help more than the other way around.

It is American power that, like a beloved '56 Chevy, seems to have passed its prime. A classic Cold War model, American centralized, militarized supremacy became so overwhelming that it defeated everything, including itself. All the components that allowed America to dominate the 20th Century are still in place – a vast economy, powerful popular culture, a big army – but the clunky way that power has been exercised under President Bush has left it looking isolated, tired, even weak. But what then will fill its space?

Many have argued that it will be a new great power like China or India. But while their economies will grow and their cultures attract more supporters, those countries suffer from the same problems as the United States: they are large, nationalistic nation states in an era of globalisation.

The new global order is being shaped in the one place where most Americans would least expect to find it: in "Old Europe". The European Union is leading a revolutionary transformation of the nature of power that in just 50 years has transformed a continent from total war to perpetual peace. By building a network of power – that binds states together with a market, common institutions, and international law – rather than a hierarchical nation-state, it is increasingly writing the rules for the 21ˢ Century.

Why Europe Matters

The reason that President Bush made the first state visit of his second term to Brussels rather than Moscow, Delhi, or Beijing is because he understood that something important is afoot. He realized that, without European diplomacy, money, and soft power, freedom's march would be a lot more halting in all the places that America cares about.

In Ukraine in December 2004, people took to the streets in search of a European Dream, and the European diplomacy of the Polish and Lithuanian Prime Ministers and EU foreign Policy Chief Javier Solana was key to sealing a peaceful end to the "Orange Revolution". In Turkey, the Government has implemented 8 legislative packages (banning the death penalty, dealing with torture in prisons, minority rights) as a precondition for its application to be part of the European club. In Sarajevo after years of humiliating failure it is a European high representative that sits over European Union forces to keep the peace. In Ramallah and Gaza it is the European Union that is training and equipping the Palestinian Police force. In Tehran, the EU's diplomacy is the world's only hope of avoiding a nuclear crisis. And in the Greater Middle East, it is the conditions attached to European aid and trade that will be the key to promoting reform. Around the world there are 70,000 European troops on peace-keeping duty.

Of course European power doesn't yet have the same global scope as the US: Brussels has little influence on North Korea or Pakistan. However, the EU's reach is constantly growing. Beyond the 450 million citizens who are already living in the EU, there are another 1.3 billion people in about 80 countries – in the former Soviet Union, the Balkans, North Africa and the Middle East and Sub-Saharan Africa – who depend on the EU for trade, finance, foreign investment and aid.

And through its ability to attract support around the world Europe is increasingly defining the rules for the world. In the last major period of global uncertainty, it was the United States that built the institutions that made the world stable – NATO, the UN, the IMF, and the World Bank. But today, the US has vacated the field and it is the European Union that has been building a post-cold war order to deal with the challenges of globalisation. Europeans pioneered the creation of the World Trade Organisation – under the leadership of the indefatigable Irishman Peter Sutherland. On climate change, after President Bush said the Kyoto Treaty was dead, Europeans ratified and implemented it. The same happened with the International Criminal Court. And when it comes to the regulation of the economy, even the mighty Microsoft marches to rules set in Brussels. Whatever the rights and wrongs of each individual regime, the need for global institutions is as great now as it was after World War II. And it is the EU that is taking the lead in building and modernising them.

In its slow and chaotic way, the EU has used the size of its market and its diplomacy to develop a different kind of power, one that I call "transformative power". This power, described in detail in the 11 chapters of this book, is the most important development in international relations since the creation of the nation state.

The Referendums and Europe's "Ross Perot Moment"

Periodically, the greatest threat to European Union seems to be vocal European disunity. No sooner had President Bush expressed his support for the European Union's proposed constitution than the French public decided to reject it. And with the Dutch following suit, many will wonder how Europe can be a player in global affairs if it can't even agree on its own constitution.

The consequences of the rejection are unsettling: they will no doubt unleash another bout of Euro-navel-gazing, and have raised important questions about the durability of Europe's institutions, the legitimacy of the European project and the future of cherished projects such as enlargement to the East. But before Euroskeptics take too much heart they should realise that neither the French nor the Dutch were rejecting Europe per se: opinion polls in both countries show that almost 90 percent want to stay in the European Union. And because of this fact, the logic behind European integration, and its revolutionary potential will not be affected in the long run.

First, it is important to realise that the rejection of the constitution creates a political rather than an institutional crisis. The European Union already has a de facto constitution with its 80,000 pages of law, its common market, single currency, and increasingly common defense force (that has served in Bosnia, Macedonia, and the Democratic Republic of the Congo). None of these things will be wiped out by the Referendum.

In many ways, the constitutional crisis is more a continuation of business as usual than a break with the past. Historians have shown us that the European Union (EU) has been in a state of crisis since its inception more than 50 years ago. France voted "No" to European defense cooperation in 1954 and vetoed British EU membership in the 1960s. Denmark dealt a blow with its nej to the 1992 Maastricht Treaty and to the single currency in 2000. The Irish rejected the Treaty of Nice in 2001, and the Swedish voted "No" to the euro in 2003. Yet, somehow the fact that all European countries need the European Union to succeed has meant that the European project has emerged stronger from every setback. There is no reason to imagine the EU won't emerge from that experience stronger once again.

Secondly, that political crisis is forcing European governments to engage with their citizens. The double "No" was in part a revolt against out-of-touch political elites, a cry against an enlargement process that had never been properly debated, and a rejection of the style of a political project that was sealed off from people's everyday lives. It was a "Ross Perot" moment for Europe.

For the pioneers of the European Coal and Steel Community in the 1950s -most importantly France and Germany – the memories of war were fresh and the European project was fragile, a bicycle that needed to be peddled constantly lest it fall over. As a result the debates in Europe were always about whether to go forward or back – rather than what kind of Europe should be built. This has meant that Europe has been built by elites without involving the citizens in a debate about its future direction.

Elections for the European Parliament have never been about the direction of Europe. Rather, they merely offered a cost-free way of punishing unpopular national governments. National elections are about health, education, jobs, and taxes – pretty much anything apart from Europe. Even previous referenda on European treaties have offered a pseudo-choice between "more" or "less" Europe, rather than acknowledging that there can be a choice between different visions of integration. The classic example of that was France's referendum on the Maastricht Treaty in 1992, when there was almost no discussion in France of the single currency's "convergence criteria," which set the all-important limits on national debt and inflation. The only question was whether you were for or against European integration.

Today, the debate over "Europe, right or wrong" is ending. That choice is being replaced by a battle between different visions of Europe. The fight is on between social integrationists who oppose enlargement and reform and liberal expansionists who see Europe doing best by looking outwards and shedding outdated institutions like the Common

Agricultural policy. This book is a contribution to that debate: a manifesto for a self-confident, outward-looking, enlarging, decentralised union that is global in its interests and sense of responsibility. It is a vision that is already winning through. In spite of the overblown rhetoric about the end of enlargement, the European Union has so far stuck to its commitments: indicating that it will stick to its commitment to start membership talks with Turkey, and admit Romania and Bulgaria, albeit on a slightly delayed timetable.

Behind the headline-capturing rows and political turmoil is a continent-wide union of nations that is expanding its reach into the world and maturing politically: that Europe will be capable of acting as a reliable and active partner to the United States. More than that, it may be a model that provides some lessons that its original sponsor could usefully follow.

Mark Leonard
London, June 2005

The Power of Weakness and the Weakness of Power: Why Europe Will Run the Twenty-First Century

In the middle of Pennsylvania Avenue in Washington a middle-aged woman with a weather-beaten face and a brown wig sits on a milk crate. Surrounded by hand-painted placards calling for nuclear disarmament, Concepcion Picciotto hands out her cheaply produced leaflets to any passer-by who will stop to listen. This remarkable woman has been holding a vigil outside the White House day and night for twenty-one years – sleeping, in a sitting position, for just three hours a night, so as to avoid breaking the stringent DC vagrancy laws. It is impossible not to be moved by her conviction and moral rectitude; it is equally impossible not to be depressed by the futility of a cause that has robbed her of the best years of her life.

It does not take long for most Americans to figure out that Concepcion is European. Like Concepcion's faith in world peace, they see Europe's belief in international institutions and the rule of international law as weak and unworldly – a luxurious delusion which post-9/11 America can no longer afford. In fact for many, Concepcion represents the distilled essence of the European position: lazy, free-riding, idealistic, and weak. She lives on American handouts of money and food, and enjoys the protection of the Washington Police Department without contributing a cent to pay for its upkeep. And yet she has the temerity to sit at the gates of the White House and complain about the manner in which her providers and protectors choose to conduct themselves.

What is more, many Europeans would agree. The conventional wisdom is that Europe's hour has come and gone. Its lack of vision, divisions, obsession with legal frameworks, unwillingness to project military power, and sclerotic economy are contrasted with a United States more dominant even than Rome at the height of the imperial republic, and not afraid to use force to get its way. We are told that if the American Empire is set to dominate the next fifty years, it is the Chinese and Indians who will take over the baton and dominate the second half of the century.

But the problem is not Europe – it is our outdated understanding of power.

The Weakness of Power

For all the talk of American Empire, the last two years have been above all else a demonstration of the limits of American power. America's economic lead over the rest of the world has disappeared (in 1950 its GDP was twice the size of Western Europe's and five times Japan's; today its GDP is the same size as the EU's and less than double that of Japan's[1]); and its political power is waning (its failure to secure support from Europeans, and even from countries as economically dependent on the USA as Mexico and Chile, showed that the price for saying no to the United States has been going down). In fact American dominance is only clear-cut on two levels: the ability to fight and win intensive conventional wars, and the ubiquity of American popular culture.[2] Joseph Nye has characterized these two kinds of power as 'hard' and 'soft': the ability to get your way by coercion and attraction.[3] Both are declining currencies.

Terrorism and weapons of mass destruction allow the desperate and weak to neutralize the superpower's military machine.[4] And by constantly talking of countries as rogue states and threatening them with military attack, the Bush Administration actually encourages them to adopt these tactics. What is more, as the administration becomes obsessed with 'Hard Power', it further erodes American 'Soft Power' by replacing memories of America as saviour with fear of the instability its war on terror is causing. As David Calleo says: 'Where promiscuous Europe sees a world where everybody is a potential friend, martial America lives in a world where every independent power is a potential enemy.'[5] The paradox is that the more this Janus-faced empire flouts its strength, the less it is able to achieve its goals on the world stage.

To understand the shape of the twenty-first century, we need a revolution in the way we think about power. The overblown rhetoric directed at the 'American Empire' misses the fact that the US reach – militarily and diplomatically – is shallow and narrow. The lonely superpower can bribe, bully, or impose its will almost anywhere in the world, but when its back is turned, its potency wanes. The strength of the EU, conversely, is broad and deep: once sucked into its sphere of influence, countries are changed forever. For fifty years, under the cover of an American security blanket, Europe has been creating a 'community of democracy' and using its market size and the promise of engagement to reshape societies from the inside. As India, Brazil, South Africa, and even China develop economically and express themselves politically, the European model will represent an irresistibly attractive way of enhancing their prosperity whilst protecting their security. They will join with the EU in building 'a New European Century'.

The Power of Weakness

If you put the words 'Europe' and 'crisis' into the internet search engine Google, over four million entries come up. Newspapers have used them together so often that they are almost interchangeable: on any day over the last fifty years there have been stories of divisions, failure to meet targets, diplomatic wrangles, a perpetual sense of failure. But historians tell a different story from journalists. They describe a continent with one of the most successful foreign policies in history. They tell us that, in just fifty years, war between European powers has become unthinkable; that European economies have caught up with America; and that Europe has brought successive waves of countries out of dictatorship and into democracy.

When they look at a map of the world, they will describe a zone of peace spreading like a blue oil slick – from the west coast of Ireland to the east of the Mediterranean; from the Arctic Circle to the Straits of Gibraltar – sucking in new members in its wake. And around this blue map of the European Union (covering over 450 million citizens) they will describe another zone of 385 million people who share land and sea borders with the EU. Surrounding them another 900 million people are umbilically linked to a European Union that is their biggest trade partner and their biggest source of credit, foreign investment, and aid. These 2 billion people (one third of the world's population) live in the 'Eurosphere': Europe's zone of influence, which is gradually being transformed by the European project and adopting European ways of doing things.[6]

Because news is told by journalists rather than historians, European power is often confused with weakness. But when a country like Russia signs the Kyoto Protocol on green-house gas emissions in order to smooth relations with the European Union; when Poland reverses decades of practice to introduce constitutional protection for ethnic minorities to be allowed to join the EU; when an Islamist government in Turkey abandons its own party's proposals for a penal code that makes adultery a crime punishable by law so as not to attract the ire of Brussels; or a right-wing Republican administration swallows hard and asks the UN for help over Iraq – then we need to question our definitions of power and weakness.

We can see that a new kind of power has evolved that cannot be measured in terms of military budgets or smart missile technology. It works in the long term, and is about reshaping the world rather than winning short-term tussles. Europe's power is a 'transformative power'.[7] And when we stop looking at the world through American eyes, we can see that each element of European 'weakness' is in fact a facet of its extraordinary 'transformative power'.

Europe doesn't flaunt its strength or talk about a 'single sustainable model of progress'. Instead, like an 'invisible hand', it operates through the shell of traditional political structures. The British House of Commons, British law courts, and British civil servants are still there, but they have all become agents of the European Union. This is no accident. By creating common standards that are implemented through national institutions, Europe can spread its influence without becoming a target for hostility. While every US company, embassy, and military base is a terrorist target, Europe's relative invisibility allows it to extend its global reach without the same provocation. The fact that Europe does not have one leader, but rather a network of centres of power united by common policies and goals, means that it can expand to accommodate ever-greater numbers of countries without collapsing, and continue to provide its members with the benefits of being the largest market in the world.

Europeans are not interested in classic geo-politics when they talk to other countries. They start from the other end of the spectrum: What values underpin the State? What are its constitutional and regulatory frameworks? Europe's obsession with legal frameworks means that it can completely transform the countries it comes into contact with, instead of just skimming the surface. The USA may have changed the regime in Afghanistan, but Europe is changing all of Polish society, from its economic policies and property laws to its treatment of minorities and what gets served on the nation's tables.

Europe doesn't change countries by threatening to invade them: its biggest threat is having nothing to do with them at all. While the EU is deeply involved in Serbia's reconstruction and supports its desire to be 'rehabilitated' as a European state, the USA offers Colombia no such hope of integration through multilateral institutions or structural funds, only the temporary 'assistance' of American military training missions and aid, and the raw freedom of the US market.

By creating the largest single internal market in the world, Europe has become an economic giant that, according to some calculations, is already the biggest in the world.[8] But it is the quality of Europe's economy that makes it a model: its low levels of inequality allow countries to save on crime and prisons; its energy-efficient economies will protect them from the hike in oil prices; its social model gives people leisure and time with their families. Europe represents a synthesis of the energy and freedom that come from liberalism with the stability and welfare that come from social democracy. As the world becomes richer and moves beyond satisfying basic needs such as hunger and health, the European way of life will become irresistible.

In every corner of the world countries are drawing inspiration from the European model and nurturing their own neighbourhood clubs. This 'regional domino effect' will change our ideas of politics, economics and redefine what power means for the twenty-first century.

The Project for a New European Century

Imagine a world of peace, prosperity, and democracy. A world where small countries are as sovereign as large ones.

A world where what matters is that you obey the law – rather than whether you are with us or against us; where your democratic values are more important than what you have done in the war on terror this week; where you can have a population of just 400,000 and be part of the biggest economy in the world. What I am asking you to imagine is the 'New European Century'.

This book is not an attempt to excuse all of Europe's faults. It has plenty: from the absurdity of its common agricultural policy to the meanness of its immigration policies; from its lack of assertiveness on the world stage to its over-assertiveness in devising standards. However, it *is* an attempt to defend the European Union from its enemies: both those who seek to hide its extraordinary achievements by blaming it – often unfairly – for all manner of evils, and those who, in the name of the European cause, want to turn it into something else: a federal state on the American model. Both these groups have succeeded in filling Europeans with gloom. My aim is to help cast off the oppressive yoke of pessimism that has enveloped our continent before it becomes a self-fulfilling prophecy.

CHAPTER 1

Europe's Invisible Hand

In the beginning there was no future, only the recent past. Blood-drenched, genocidal, and everywhere. The bodies had piled up with each new vision of European unity: 184,000 in the Franco-Prussian War, 8 million in the First World War, 40 million in the Second World War.[1] Grand plans and charisma had almost extinguished a continent. It needed a miracle to recover, but Europe could not bring itself to believe in romantic leadership again. With six words the French poet Paul Valéry captured the European condition in 1945: 'We hope vaguely, we dread precisely.'[2]

That is why Europe's epic escape from history was guided not by the larger-than-life heroes of the war – people like Churchill or De Gaulle, who inspired a generation to fight – but by a group of almost anonymous technocrats who were dedicated to taking the gun out of Europe's future. The key figure was Jean Monnet, a small, unprepossessing, stocky French official, who reminded the journalist Anthony Sampson unavoidably of Agatha Christie's Hercule Poirot.

Monnet's contribution was a vision of how not to have a vision. He took Valéry's observation and turned it into a dictum for the organization of Europe. He let the fear of conflict drive European unity and left its goal vague, allowing everyone to feel that Europe was going their way. To this day, Europe is a journey with no final destination, a political system that shies away from the grand plans and concrete certainties that define American politics. Its lack of vision is the key to its strength.

Monnet's first principle was to avoid blueprints. The 'Schuman Declaration', which the French and the Germans signed to launch the European project in 1950, makes the lack of plans a cardinal principle: 'Europe will not be made all at once, or according to a single general plan. It will be built through concrete achievements, which first create a *de facto* solidarity.'[3] Monnet had worked in the disastrous League of Nations after the First World War and understood the need to start with concrete forms of co-operation rather than an illusory idea of the international community. He tried to bind France and Germany together by uniting the production of coal and steel: the industries that had built the weapons of war would now provide the foundations for peace. Monnet's tactic was always to focus on technical details rather than the big political questions that attract headlines. He tried to tackle contentious issues by breaking them down into component parts – it is a lot easier to get agreement on coal and steel tariffs than war and peace. And once the governments of France and Germany were sucked into endless negotiations, they were less likely to go to war.

The best way to change the facts on the ground was through gradual change – what Monnet called *engrenage*.

Each agreement to co-operate at a European level would lead inexorably to another agreement that deepened European integration. Once Europe's leaders had agreed to remove tariffs, they focused on non-tariff barriers such as regulations, health and safety standards, and qualifications. When many of the non-tariff barriers had been addressed by the creation of a single market, Europe's leaders focused on the single currency. Wider and wider groups of politicians and civil servants now had a stake in European integration. Thousands of meetings took place between officials from different governments, which meant, quite simply, that they got to know each other very well. They would therefore think spontaneously of other things they could do together.

Monnet's bizarre working practices set a pattern that the European Union's workings would follow. Stanley Cleveland, one of Monnet's disciples, describes his method:

> Whenever Monnet attacked a new problem he would gather a bunch of people around him ... He would begin a sort of non-stop *Kaffeeklatsch*. It could go on sometimes for a period of one or two weeks – hours and hours a day ... Monnet would remain silent, occasionally provoking reaction, but not saying much ... Then gradually, as the conversation developed – and it often took several days or even a week before this happened – he began venturing a little statement of his own. [4]

Monnet would start with a very simple statement, almost a slogan, to see how his companions reacted. He would then expose a little more of his thinking, turning the slogan into a few sentences and then a couple of paragraphs. As his companions objected and told him what was wrong with what he said, he would reformulate his ideas until they were acceptable to everyone in the discussion. Monnet would produce up to thirty drafts of a memorandum, speech, or proposal. The purpose of this constant iteration is identical with the purpose of the EU's current never-ending process of policy formulation, negotiation, and review: to remove any and all conflicts or obstacles around an issue. The product would be an outward simplicity for a complex idea.

What Monnet created was a machine of political alchemy. Each country would follow its national interest, but once the different national interests were put into the black box of European integration, a European project would emerge at the other end. For the Benelux countries, the Second World War had drastically exposed their vulnerability to the big powers in Europe, so they needed to find a way of reining in France and Germany; but also, as small European powers, their only real prospect of exercising influence was through some kind of unified inter-state system. For Germany, and also to an extent Italy, the major goal was political rehabilitation from their position as pariah states. Membership of a European community also represented a buttress against the threat from the East, and an opportunity to get rid of the allied market restrictions that prevented the necessary access to markets for Germany to rebuild. For France, German containment was the key goal, backed up by the prospects for economic growth which access to German markets and productive capacity offered – what Jacques Delors described as the marriage contract on which the EEC was founded.[5]

All of these were calculations of national interest, and yet the outcome of their filtering through Monnet's European institutions was a solution to the problem of European conflict.[6] In Europe today, war is not simply undesirable – it is inconceivable. The founder of liberal economics, Adam Smith, developed the evocative idea of the 'invisible hand' of the market to explain how a system of perfect liberty, operating under the drives and constraint of human nature and intelligently designed institutions, would give rise to an orderly society rather than a 'war of all against all'.[7] In many ways, Monnet's genius was to develop a 'European invisible hand' that allows an orderly European society to emerge from each country's national interest.[8] And that is possibly the most powerful element of Monnet's vision: he did not try to abolish the nation-state or nationalism – simply to change its nature by pooling sovereignty.

Europe has been able to extend itself into the lives of Europeans largely unchallenged by seeping into the existing structure of national life, leaving national institutions outwardly intact but inwardly transformed. The 'Europeanization' of national political life has largely gone on behind the scenes, but its very invisibility has seen the triumph of a unique political experiment.

The Invisible Political System

The Palace of Westminster, London. It is 11.30 a.m. on a Thursday and the Secretary of State for Agriculture, Margaret Beckett, is preparing to take questions – just as her predecessors have done for three hundred years. The daily prayers have been said and MPs are settling down on their green benches – behind the sword-lines that were originally introduced to stop the opposing front benches from stabbing each other while they spoke. The MPs are tired and anxious to get off to their constituencies so the chorus of 'Hear, Hear' and the waving of order papers is even louder than usual.

Although the trappings of 'Question Time' have not changed in centuries, this façade of continuity hides the fact that over half of British agricultural legislation is made to implement decisions taken by our ministers in Brussels.[9] Although the House of Commons can hold Margaret Beckett to account, the key decisions are not made by her alone. Instead they are made in negotiations with her counterparts in gatherings of European agriculture ministers and the various technical committees that meet between three and four hundred times a year.[10] But for a visitor to the House of Commons, or even a British farmer, nothing has changed because the policies are not implemented or ratified at a European level. The farmer will continue to deal with the national Ministry of Agriculture, the national customs and excise authorities, the national vets and health and safety executives who have become the custodians of European policy.

This invisible Europeanization of power is happening across the spectrum of British politics. There is no longer a single national ministry that has not met with its counterparts in some EU forum or another, including defence ministers, transport ministers, and even home affairs ministers. The best estimates are that up to a third of British legislation and two-thirds of economic and social legislation are made by British ministers with their European colleagues in Brussels.[11]

While Europe has seeped into the bloodstream of national

politics, it is careful to take a back seat. It is the House of Commons, national civil servants, and national law courts that ratify and implement European decisions. Because national governments are the agents of European power, the European Commission can remain small and discreet. The European Commission has a total staff of 22,000 – less than many large city councils. This gives it barely half a civil servant per 10,000 citizens, as against 300 per 10,000 on average for the national civil services.[12] Some Eurosceptics have unfairly argued that Europe is a stealthy federalist project. In fact, every single step has been voluntary and has been debated and agreed by national parliaments. It is, however, deliberately low profile so that its builders focus on making policy work rather than political grandstanding.

The European Union is about enhancing rather than destroying national identities. Brussels, the antithesis of an imperial capital, is in many ways a microcosm of Europe, representing and encapsulating European history. Almost every invasion and political project – from the Roman Empire, through Napoleon to the Third Reich – has come through and absorbed it. And today its population, architecture, and ideology is a haphazard over-layering of their legacies. A third of its population is foreign[13] (with the rootless, well-paid elite of Eurocrats living side by side with the socially excluded immigrants of European empires past, Moroccans, Congolese, Rwandans). It is the capital of a country with no real sense of national identity (and a constant jockeying for position between the Walloons and Flemings who inhabit it).

The expat's burden of carrying his home in his head means that there is no risk of going native. Few of the Eurocrats who move to Brussels even try to fit in. Many of the British cling to their roots by recreating a little England. Despite living in one of the culinary capitals of Europe, they fill their cupboards and fridges with pre-packaged, ready-made parcels of home: Bird's custard powder, Walkers crisps, Heinz baked beans, Wall's sausages, and Savlon cream. And this is nothing compared with the patriotic fervour of the Greeks, who kit themselves out in fancy dress and dance through the streets on their national holiday. Or the Irish, whose legendary St Patrick's Day celebrations spill out of the dozens of Irish pubs that are scattered around the city. Brussels is an unobtrusive vessel that allows powerful national identities to flourish – the living embodiment of the British Conservative Party sound-bite of being 'in Europe, not run by it'.

By keeping a low profile at home and working through national structures, Europe has managed to spread its wings without attracting much hostility. As it becomes a force to be reckoned with on the world stage, it can act in the same way. When European troops go overseas they rarely wear European uniforms. They often serve under the flags of NATO or the United Nations. Where Europe has established protectorates, such as in Bosnia and Kosovo, its special representatives do so in the name of the United Nations as well as the European Union.

European power even has a low profile in the economic sphere. The EU economy is the same size as that of the USA, with comparable levels of capital investment in the economies of other countries, and yet that economic muscle – in many respects greater than that of the USA – just isn't noticed in the same way. Anti-globalization is almost exclusively an anti-American phenomenon, even within the USA itself, when its antithesis, globalization, is just as much a European phenomenon. The intrusion of McDonald's provokes the bile of economic nationalists and opponents of globalization everywhere. All of that movement's hate figures – Starbucks, Gap, Nike – are universally identified as American companies. In some respects, the attack on the World Trade Center demonstrates this paradox – an attack on the heart of the global economy naturally took place in New York because American economic might is so blatant. Europe's comparable might simply lacks that profile.

This even extends to America's occasional fears of a foreign economic takeover within the USA. The 1980s saw remarkable levels of nail-biting and hand-wringing within the USA over the rise of Japan and its putative takeover of the commanding heights of the US economy. European investment in the USA now easily surpasses that of Japan, yet it barely merits a mention in American analysts' dissections of European weakness.

The most obvious reason for Europe's invisibility abroad is the dark episode of European colonial history that means there is a real reluctance in Europe to adopt the trappings of empire. But there is a deeper reason for this respect for local cultures. The European vision has never aimed to establish a single model of human progress: it is about allowing diverse and competing cultures to live together in peace. This was captured most dramatically when the Northern Irish politician John Hume was given the Nobel Peace Prize. In his acceptance speech he talked of the European Union as the most successful peace process in history: 'The European visionaries demonstrated that difference is not a threat, difference is natural ... The answer to difference is to respect it ... The peoples of Europe created institutions which respected their diversity – a Council of Ministers, the European Commission and the European Parliament – but allowed them to work together in their common and substantial economic interest.'[14]

This diversity also has the unexpected effect of making the European Union stick to its principles. An example illustrates this well. When the Berlin Wall fell in 1989, there was no agreement on which former Communist countries to let into the club. Because Europe's leaders failed to agree on the final borders of the European Union they decided to make entry open to anyone who met the 'Copenhagen Criteria of democracy, the rule of law, and economic liberalism. Lurking in the background of this decision was a desire to exclude some countries. Several member-states were particularly keen to use the agreement to lift the bar of membership so high that Turkey would never be able to join, creating tough standards on human rights and respect for minorities that they felt would remain beyond the Kemalist republic's reach. However, these very criteria have driven Turkey to reform itself, and they will pave the way for a modern and democratic Turkey to join (despite the lack of enthusiasm for Turkish membership from many EU members). The same happened with the Maastricht convergence criteria for monetary union – designed at least in part to keep the profligate Italians at bay – which had the effect of ending Italy's profligacy and allowing it to join.

In all of these cases, member-states have struggled to agree on their final destination and taken refuge behind processes which reflect European values. Ironically, they have chosen to project their values to the European level in order to defend their interests at a national one. This creates a strange situation where nations have interests and no values and the EU has values but no interests.

Jean Monnet's prediction at the outset of the European project was that, 'We are starting a process of continuous reform which can shape tomorrow's world more lastingly than the priciples of revolution so widespread outside the West.'[15] But because the European project is at best half-glimpsed, hidden behind national legislatures and national executives, it is easy to miss. To the naked eye, power has not moved from the governments that remain the seat of legitimacy, and politics continues in the age-old ways. Ironically this very invisibility has allowed the European project to spread so far and so fast, creating an inexorable momentum for its own development. By coming together and pooling their sover-eignty to achieve common goals, the countries of the European Union have created new power out of nothing. The silent revolution they have unleashed will transform the world.

CHAPTER 2

'Divided We Stand, United We Fall'

1968 was a year of revolutions. What started in the Sorbonne in Paris as a protest about an outdated curriculum and the threat of a reduction in student numbers soon spread like wildfire around Europe and the United States. But the excitement was not limited to universities. Dee Hock, a middle manager in a bank in Seattle who had dropped out of community college after just two years, was starting a revolution of his own – one that could hold some important lessons for the European Union. Many have argued that Europe's divisions will stop it punching its weight in the world, but Hock's example shows that you can take over the world without developing a centralized bureaucracy.

Hock's journey started when the bank's headquarters appointed him to a committee that was working on a business strategy for its ailing credit card, Bankamericard. The backdrop was bleak. Credit cards had only existed for ten years and the infant industry was in chaos. Banks had dropped millions of unsolicited cards on an unsuspecting public that had no experience of credit facilities of this kind. Losses were thought to be in the hundreds of millions of dollars. Card owners were bankrupted, politicians were alarmed, and the media launched a feeding frenzy of blame-calling.

Instead of developing a new business strategy, Hock persuaded his superiors to start a new kind of organization: Visa. He was determined to move beyond the hierarchical companies that were products of the industrial revolution and create an organization based on biological concepts – a network. He wanted to create a franchise that would have global presence, but maintain competition between individual banks so that they would be driven to innovate.

The basic principle was to create a company that did not have shareholders but members. These members would own the company for ever but could not buy or sell their part of the company – which meant that it would be impossible for any individual member to gain control of the overall organization. Hock wanted to create an organization that would be both highly decentralized and highly collaborative. Authority, initiative, decision making, wealth – everything possible was pushed out to the periphery of the organization, to the members. What began with just a handful of modest banks in just twelve states grew into an organization that is now owned by over 21,000 financial institutions in 150 countries. Today Visa is responsible for the largest single block of consumer spending ($2.7 trillion annually), services 600 million people, and continues to grow at a rate of 22 per cent a year.[1]

In spite of its enormous economic power, Visa is effectively a skeletal organization with a tiny central administration and only three thousand employees in twenty-one offices around the world. It relies for its strength and success on enabling others to flourish. And that, says Hock, is exactly how it ought to be. 'The better an organization is, the less obvious it is,' he says. 'In Visa, we tried to create an invisible organization and keep it that way. It's the results, not the structure or management that should be apparent.'[2]

Network Europe

Although he predated Dee Hock and came from a very different world, the principles that Monnet promoted bear a remarkable resemblance to those that have turned Visa into one of the most successful companies in global history. Though very few people realize it, the European Union he gave birth to is already closer to Visa than it is to a state: it is a decentralised network that is owned by its member-states.[3]

The headquarters of the EU Council says it all. The Justus Lipsius Building looks like it has landed in Brussels from outer-space – obliterating the genteel Art-Deco surroundings with its marble footprint. Clad in heavy grey stone and reflective glass, this anonymous rectangular building covers some 215,000 square metres, circling a mammoth atrium with 24 kilometres-worth of corridors of power.[4] Like a Russian doll, the external shell has replicated itself infinitely inside, housing dozens of rectangular rooms – each containing a rectangular table with a hole in the middle. The tables are neatly set up for European negotiations with place-names for the twenty-five member-states, long, thin microphones, notepads, and bunches of red pencils. In some of the rooms there are booths for interpreters to translate between the twenty EU languages. This building is like a factory for European agreements. And because the EU is a network rather than a state, negotiation is not a part-time activity: it goes on every single day, around the clock. Like the banks that own and control Visa, it is the national governments that set the agenda for the future of Europe.

Four times a year, all the EU Heads of Government gather here amid a fanfare of publicity, with a media party that runs to the thousands. There are between 80 and 90 meetings a year[5] of various formations of the Council of Ministers, which brings national ministers (agriculture ministers, finance ministers, health ministers, etc) together to agree policies in each of their areas. Working under the ministers are groups of national civil servants. The 'Committee of Permanent Representatives', made up of ambassadors from all the member-states, is responsible for agreeing 90 per cent of the European Union's legislation.[6] Working under it are dozens of 'working groups' that prepare agreements in each of the different policy areas.

The process is complicated, but it allows every country or parliament in the network to have some say. Before decisions even reach the magic circle in Brussels, national parliaments can mandate their governments to stick to a clear national position. After decisions have been taken, they then face a tough process of scrutiny from the 723 directly elected members of the European Parliament who represent citizens from the twenty-five member-states.[7] Finally, the laws that are agreed are upheld by the European Court of Justice, made up of judges appointed from all the member-states and which acts as a supreme court.

In seminar rooms across the world, historians and political scientists are trying to understand and categorize the European Union. The usual parlour game is to guess which country the EU will end up copying. Will it be the USA – perhaps the 1850s confederal model? Or will it be a constitutional federal democracy like post-war Germany, or the Swiss system where national political debates are much less important than local scuffles and the needs of the secretive banking economy? Some predict an overpowering bureaucratic state on the Napoleonic model, while others fear we will build a political system so divided that it could collapse like the French Fourth Republic. Some Americans, in particular, are impatient for the Union to unite; to develop a federal structure; to have a constitution that clearly separates the executive, judiciary, and legislature; to elect a single president; and to give the European Parliament law-making powers like national parliaments. In short, to get a 'single phone number'.[8] But Jean Monnet's genius was to create a political structure that is quite different from the traditional nation-state.

Although some federalists still dream of a country called Europe, and the European Union sometimes pretends to be a state with its flag, passport, and anthem, it is fundamentally different from a state. Like Visa, it is a decentralized network that exists to serve its member-states. The EU is a skeletal organization that leaves the real power to its member-states, which are responsible for implementing and overseeing the vast majority of the European Union's activities. This revolutionary structure has allowed the European Union to grow with the support of its members. But it has also fundamentally changed the nature of global politics.

Reversing the Balance of Power

If Europe's peaceful twenty-first century will benefit from the wisdom of an American banker, the horrors of the first of half of the twentieth century can be traced back to a banker from Italy. The man in question was Lorenzo de' Medici, whose family ran Florence in the fifteenth century. At that time it was one of five city-states that dominated the Italian peninsula – along with Rome, Naples, Venice, and Milan. These cities were immensely wealthy and in perpetual competition: at that time Florence had a higher annual income than the King of England, while Venice's revenue was double that of England and Spain.[9] In 1454, Francesco Sforza, the ruler of Milan, approached de' Medici to propose an alliance between their two states. He wanted to gang up on Venice before it grew too powerful. De' Medici agreed, but insisted that they must not destroy Venice as one day its power might itself be needed to stop Rome. His reply contained the historic phrase: 'the affairs of Italy must be kept in balance'. He is credited with being the first person to talk explicitly of a 'balance' of power, a principle that became one of the key foundations of European order (or disorder) for five hundred years.[10] The system was based on the mechanical idea that groups of states needed to be brought into equilibrium – like the scales that bankers used to measure gold – so that no single one could dominate the continent.

Europe's invention of small nation-states – and a system to stop any one of them overpowering the others to create an empire – was a mixed blessing. The fierce competition between them spurred them on to develop the most advanced technology in the world, and allowed a continent that was a sleepy backwater to overtake the empires of the East and assume global dominance.[11] But the logic of the balance of power was also perpetual war: the Thirty Years War, the Franco-German War, the First World War, the Second World War, and the Cold War were all fought to stop any one country rising to hegemony.

All that has now come to an end in Europe. No one fears a rising Germany or France because all the countries of Europe have formed themselves into a network that is bound together by laws and regulations.[12] Instead of competing with each other to build up arsenals of weapons or build regional alliances, their interests are defended through mutual vulnerability, pooled sovereignty, and transparency. But outside the warm womb of the European Union, the balance of power lives on: between India and Pakistan, in the Middle East, in Central Asia, and the Far East.

Although these countries are all trying to balance each other, no one is trying to check Europe's rise. In fact, Europe has even managed to reverse the very idea of the balance of power. As its strength grows, it is becoming a powerful magnet for its neighbours who want to join it rather than balance it. The American political economist Richard Rosecrance has shown that this is the first time in history that a great power has arisen without provoking other countries to unite against it. In a remarkable survey of the formation of empires and states he shows how every major power from Spain in the sixteenth century through France, Britain, and the United States in the nineteenth century to Germany, Japan, and the Soviet Union in the twentieth century and the USA in the twenty-first century has provoked its neighbours to unite against it.[13] So why has Europe managed to become more united and powerful without attracting hostility?

One argument is that Europe is an economic rather than a political superpower. Walter Russell Mead argues that economic might draws people in while political power creates hostility. He explains this theory by comparing economic power to the carnivorous sundew plant: 'a pleasing scent lures insects towards its sap. But once the victim has touched the sap, it is stuck; it can't get away. That is sticky power; that is how economic power works.'[14] There is something in the claim that economic power doesn't create the same fears in its neighbours as political power, but it does not explain why the United States, China, Russia, and India look more benignly on the growth of the European economy than they do on each other's economic development. There is an entire industry of US foreign policy thinking based on the need to balance China's growing economic power, even though by some definitions its economy is still smaller than Italy's, but there is very little concern about a European Union whose economy is the largest in the world.

The most compelling explanation comes from the unique nature of the European Union: as a network rather than a state. International relations scholars have compared the relationship between states to billiard balls on a table. They have a hard shell and repel each other when they clash. But while it is easy to clash with another state, it is difficult to clash with a network that is made up of a cacophony of different voices. The point of a network – or club – is that it doesn't have a hard centre like a billiard ball, so when you try to balance it, you are often sucked into a process of engagement with its different members. The most surprising example of this was the crisis in Iraq.

The Beast with Twenty-Five Heads

There are few creatures more potent in Greek mythology than the Hydra, a beast with the body of a serpent and nine heads. Each time you chopped one head off, two others would grow in its place. With its many member-states, the EU is like a modern day hydra – as Colin Powell discovered when he tried to build an international coalition for invading Iraq. Each time he managed to sign one country up, he found another one still had doubts. In the immediate aftermath of the invasion, the conventional wisdom was that the Americans had won – dividing the European countries and prevailing on some of them to invade Iraq on American terms, without a United Nations mandate and against the wishes of a majority of European citizens. A headline in the *Financial Times* on 12 March 2003, as troops prepared to invade Iraq, seemed to say it all: 'Europe is the first casualty of war.'[15]

Most people think that Iraq was a disaster for Europe, and I shared their distress at the political fall-out from the crisis. But with hindsight we can see that some good came out of it. The European project has survived the transatlantic train crash, and its multilateral agenda has in fact made a come-back. Though the Continent was divided on tactics for handling the United States, all EU countries shared three fundamental goals: to preserve the transatlantic alliance, to restore the authority of the United Nations, and to prevent unilateral preventive war from being established as a norm. Europe has somehow met all these objectives – not by putting up a united front, but by engaging the Americans with competing factions. The negotiations in the run-up to the war

29

were reminiscent of the routines in so many Hollywood detective movies where the 'bad cop' scares the suspect into submission, while the 'good cop' wins his trust. Between them they manage to get him to confess.

In 2003, the transatlantic relationship seemed as if it was on the cusp of being discarded when the American Defense Secretary, Donald Rumsfeld, grouped Germany with 'problem states' like Iran and Libya and Germany's justice minister compared George W. Bush to Hitler. Robert Kagan's fashionable thesis that Europe and the United States were two tectonic plates inevitably moving apart seemed irrefutable.[16] In retrospect, however, the fact that some European countries supported the war meant that the transatlantic relationship survived. As long as Bush needed Blair alongside him, there was at least an incentive for America not to be too destructive towards a political project valued by the British government.

The United Nations was sidelined and mocked during the 1990s – powerless in the face of civilian massacres in Rwanda and Somalia, ignored over Kosovo, and starved of dues by big donors. But during the run-up to the Iraq war it became the crucible in which the arguments were aired and decisions on the basis for war were made. For the first time since the Cuban missile crisis, dramatic presentations at the United Nations dominated the media, and international public opinion rallied to its cause. Now the United States has turned to the United Nations to give credibility to the beleaguered Iraqi Governing Council – not something that would have seemed likely at the time of the invasion.

Most importantly, the doctrine of preventive war seems to have disappeared into the desert sands. The US national security strategy had outlined a doctrine of war that would allow the USA to attack potential enemies *before* they posed a direct threat to US security. At their most hubristic, the neo-conservatives argued that the USA could take advantage of its victory in Iraq by unleashing a 'democratic domino effect' in Iran and Syria. The political and economic costs of invading Iraq make another occupation impossible for several years. France and Germany have made any future action harder by refusing to commit troops to Iraq or pay for reconstruction.

This success was a direct result of Europe's structure. While the US administration was pursuing its policy of divide and rule – and talking separately to each of the Hydra's heads – the European heads were busy watching each other and adapting their positions accordingly. There was certainly no 'grand plan' behind the approach of individual countries and, as the crisis reached its apotheosis, there was very little dialogue between the competing camps; but the actions of each European government were carried out in the knowledge of what the other camps were doing. The French and Germans could only afford to take a very aggressive approach because they knew that the 'New Europe' led by Blair, Aznar, Miller, and Berlusconi would stay on good terms with Bush. Equally, Tony Blair knew that, however far he went to support American action, it was likely that this would be a one-off that would not be repeated in Iran or Syria because of the depth of opposition in France and Germany. The fact that the European powers had such a strong consensus on the strategic goals – of Atlanticism, support for international law, and opposition to unilateral preventive war – meant that without any formal attempt to co-ordinate their positions, it was likely that these principles would shine through.

The European Union does not just have a 'good cop' and a 'bad cop': it is like an entire police force of good and bad cops. Other countries will always be able to find someone in the European system who is more sympathetic to their cause, and this will tend to draw them into a process of negotiation from which it is often hard to escape. The 'good cops' will then often hide behind the 'bad cops' in the EU system and manage to extract concessions. For example, British and Nordic enthusiasm for enlargement to the East allowed the countries of Central and Eastern Europe to 'keep faith' as they embarked on painful processes of internal reform. At the same time, French doubts allowed the European Commission to exact concessions from them in the protracted negotiations for accession. The key feature of this 'good cop, bad cop' dynamic is that, even though the disagreements are genuine, the core objectives of all European countries tend to be the same: a commitment to multilateral action; democracy, human rights and the international rule of law; negotiation and engagement rather than military force. Therefore, countries that seek to play Europeans off against each other tend to get pulled back to these basic principles.

However, in spite of all this success, many Euro-enthusiasts are not advocates for 'Network Europe'. Even those who concede that the network works well for economic policy, because like Visa it gives its members access to economies of scale without removing the competition that drives inno-vation, will say it is hopeless for foreign policy. But as we have seen, the development of 'Network Europe' has paradoxically allowed the EU to become a global power to be reckoned with, not just ending the balance of power in its own backyard, but reversing it.

Our 'Network Europe' has not come about as a result of a conscious plan. It is the product of an uneasy truce between the traditional visions of a European superstate and a European free-trade area – but no single vision has managed to achieve unanimous support. And it never will. As Europe develops in the future, we must embrace its unique structure, and reform it to make it work to our advantage.

Of course, we need to get better at managing the divisions within Europe. The wounds inflicted by the Iraqi disagreements run deep, and Europe cannot afford to rip itself apart every time a major international issue arises. One lesson from the Iraq war is that Europeans can have greater influence if they develop a common position before a crisis erupts, as they have done towards Iran. However, we must recognize that the persistence of different views is a strength rather than a weakness, and that the EU's structure is robust enough to accommodate disagreements of monumental proportions. Samuel Beckett said that if at first you don't succeed 'Fail, fail again, fail better'. The genius of Europe is that it carries on trying. And from every setback it has emerged stronger.

CHAPTER 3

Europe's Weapon is the Law

The bland features of Hans Blix became an unlikely fixture on our television screens and in our newspapers in early 2003. With his weapons inspections, this softly spoken balding former diplomat became the personification of hope and peace. The other familiar figure in those tense few months was Donald Rumsfeld, the ebullient American Secretary of Defense. The former wrestling champion also promised to destroy the Iraqi will to fight: not by relying on inspections, but using 'shock and awe' to scare Iraqis into submission.

The conflict went beyond the situation in Iraq. The two men became archetypes for different worldviews: the pyrotechnic might of the United States military was the perfect foil to the United Nation's preference for inspections. One offered to contain the Iraqis by spectacular displays of power, the other by keeping them under constant surveillance.

Unfortunately, spectacle and surveillance were just two sides of the same impotence, because both attempted to control Iraq from the outside. Unlike Europe's transformative power, which changes countries permanently, this kind of power lasts only as long as there is a crisis and huge amounts of international pressure and resources. As soon as the media and the political circus move on, the problems return.

The Bush Administration has used the crisis in Iraq to show that Europe's obsession with international law is a sign of its terminal weakness. It depicts it as a modern-day Prometheus bound up in red tape, at the mercy of devouring predators. But what was it that transformed Europe from being an incubator for world wars into a transmission belt for peace and democracy? The simple answer is: international law. The law is Europe's weapon of choice in its campaign to re-shape the world.

Power as Spectacle

Machiavelli famously said that it is better to be feared than to be loved. But he also warned that it is vital not to be hated. Donald Rumsfeld ignored the second part of this injunction when he ordered the Pentagon to implement the principle of 'Shock and Awe'. The report by the National Defense University, which coined the term, called for displays of firepower so dramatic that they would sap America's enemies' will to fight in the same way that the nuclear bomb had worked on Japanese fighters in Hiroshima and Nagasaki in the Second World War. [1] In an age of terror, Rumsfeld and his colleagues were looking to turn the tables on their enemies. They would use violence not to achieve specific objectives such as conquering a town or destroying a weapons factory, but as an end in itself: an instrument to enforce discipline on 'tyrants and terrorists' around the world.

This was part of a broader strategy to respond to a post-9/11 world in which terrorists could procure weapons of mass destruction from 'rogue states'. Pre-emptive strikes were intended to help restore the viability of deterrence – by making it clear that the USA would severely punish any state that considered sharing destructive technologies with terrorists. By making an example of Iraq, Rumsfeld hoped to be able to send a message to Iran, Syria, North Korea, and any other country thinking of equipping itself with weapons of mass destruction.

Using brute force to convey a message is not new. But now this idea of 'power as spectacle' can be perfected with the technology of the twenty-first century: 'daisy cutters', 'bunker-busting' nuclear bombs, squadrons of F16s, and the like. The problem with expressive violence is that its effects soon wear off. Rulers in the past found that they needed to up the ante with ever more gruesome executions and other displays of might, such as the gut-wrenching execution of Robert-François Damiens, who was ripped apart by four galloping horses for attempting to kill Louis XV of France in 1757. And even if fear can be maintained, it becomes increasingly expensive and ultimately counter-productive as it creates resentment among the very people it is seeking to control.

That is what has happened with Iraq. There were almost monthly displays of firepower between 1991 and 2003 to keep the regime on its toes. When this was felt to be failing, the logic of the allies' position compelled them to invade in 2003. The initial effect was successful. Saddam was removed, and Iran, Syria and Libya were initially cowed by the brute force of the invasion. But soon the effects wore off. Already the regimes in Tehran and Damascus feel emboldened by the fact that 130,000 US troops are bogged down in Iraq. And as the continued presence of foreign forces acts as a magnet for insurgency, the Syrian and Iranian regimes look on with relief at the transformation of a potentially popular war of liberation into an unpopular and bloody occupation.

However, the fatal flaw of 'power as spectacle' is that it is essentially destructive. It can stop people doing bad things, but it is not a good way to build and govern a complex society. In Afghanistan the allied invasion had no trouble removing the Taliban regime, but the allies failed to rebuild Afghanistan from the roots up. In spite of a veneer of democracy, the underlying realities of rule by warlords, corruption, and nepotism remain the same. As one American soldier wryly put it: 'We thought we had bought the Northern Alliance, but it turns out that we had rented them.' Once the superpower's attention had been diverted by the war in Iraq, its power to transform the Afghan Republic began to wane.

This kind of power is inefficient because it is always imposed on unwilling subjects from outside, rather than changing the wiring of society from the inside. This is what led modern societies to move from 'power as spectacle' towards 'power as surveillance'.

Power as Surveillance

The French philosopher Michel Foucault showed how, from the nineteenth century, advanced societies moved from relying largely on the deterrence of visible expressions of might to discipline enforced by making potential subjects of power visible, through regulation, official papers, CCTV and prisons. Foucault argues that the shift from spectacle to surveillance allowed modern societies to be policed at a fraction of the cost of the 'Ancien Régime'. The key was finding ways to record and monitor the behaviour of citizens in a systematic way through the development of timetables, identity cards, photographs, medical records, and laws.

The United Nation's weapons inspections were developed because military power is expensive and short-lived in its effects. By getting the international community to insist that Iraq complied with treaties that Saddam himself had signed, the UN felt that it would have the legitimacy to change Iraq. And by sending Hans Blix and Mohammed Al Baradei to triple-check every single Iraqi claim, they knew they would not have to take Saddam at his word. Weapons inspections are the direct opposite of power as spectacle: it is not the strength of Blix and his team that needs to be on show, but the behaviour of the Iraq regime and sites they are inspecting. This was power as surveillance.

And what's more, it worked – for a while at least. With hindsight we can see that while the British and American security services spectacularly failed to understand what was going on in Iraq, the UN weapons inspectors had been getting it right. Between 1991 and 1998, the inspectors destroyed almost all of Iraq's chemical and biological weapons, as well as uncovering covert transactions between Iraq and over five hundred companies from more than forty countries. In the four months that the inspectors had to verify Iraqi claims before the war, they managed to find out more than all the world's intelligence agencies.[2]

However, the UN's policy of surveillance in Iraq did depend on the spectre of US power. Without the first invasion of Iraq in 1991 the UNSCOM teams would never have been allowed in. And without the threat of the second invasion, Hans Blix would never have had the authority to hold the Iraqis to account. The problem with the UN model is that it replaces an external threat of force with the external threat of surveillance. While sending inspectors is preferable to dropping bombs, they will still be unable to change the nature of the regime and, more importantly, of the society.

Foucault's real insight is that efficient exercise of power depends less on having military might or the technology of deterrence than on establishing legitimacy by making everyone complicit in the enforcement rules. His metaphor for the rise of the 'surveillance society' is a prison called the 'Panopticon', designed by the eccentric founder of utilitarian philosophy, Jeremy Bentham. Bentham's prison was a circular building with open cells arranged in a ring around a central pillar where a guard could sit. The guard sits behind one-way blinds so that he can look out at the cells, but the inmates cannot look in. At any time, the guard may or may not be looking at an individual cell, so the prisoners have to assume that they are being watched the whole time. In other words, even when the guard is not watching them, they must behave as if he is. A vast prison with dozens of cells can thus be supervised by a single guard. Each prisoner effectively becomes his own warder, the agent of his own surveillance.[3] Once this happens, the prison guard becomes superfluous as the prison effectively polices itself.

But the inspections in Iraq were not like the surveillance of the Panopticon. They were intrusive and imposed on an uncooperative Iraqi state. Hans Blix was like a single guard policing an enormous prison that had not internalized the international community's rules. To get the Iraqis to obey the rules, the United Nations would have had to approach Iraq with a more radical idea of surveillance. This model of surveillance is what the European Union has achieved within its borders.

Europe as the Surveillance Society

The European project is based on a desire to move beyond a world of power politics, where 'might makes right', to a community based on the rule of law. Europeans have used this desire to turn a lot of the basic rules of sovereignty on their head. Until the European Union was created, the idea of statehood, of being 'sovereign', meant independence from external intervention, maintaining your secrecy, keeping other countries at bay. But, as Robert Cooper argues, instead of jealously guarding their sovereignty from external interference, Europeans have turned mutual interference and surveillance into the basis of their security.

What Europeans have done is to turn the relationship between nations in the European community into domestic policy. Over the last fifty years Europe's leaders have agreed to thousands of common standards, laws, and regulations. Together they fill thirty-one volumes and some 80,000 pages of text that regulate every facet of daily life – from human rights to consumer protection. They are known as the *acquis communitaire* – which literally means the 'aquired fortune' or 'accepted fact' of the community.

These laws work not because there is a European police state that will enforce them on recalcitrant countries that do not implement them, but because all European states want the system to succeed. Because each member state wants its fellow members to obey the law, they are forced to obey it themselves. Many people have complained about European 'red tape'; but paradoxically it is the size of Europe's body of laws that allows its institutions to be small.

This was captured by the first President of the European Commission who argued that the law is Europe's strongest weapon: 'The Community is a creature of the law, based on international treaties ... The Community has no direct means of enforcing its authority; it has neither an army nor a police force. It has only a small administrative machine and even for this purpose it must rely to a large extent on the Member States.'[4] As we have already seen, the institutions of the European Union are relatively invisible, but European power is exercised through a process of surveillance in which politicians, civil servants, and citizens internalize European power and become agents of European integration. The big challenge for Europe now is to show how this vision of order can be exported beyond Europe's member states.

Expanding the Reach of European Law

When Communism collapsed in Central and Eastern Europe, the best and the brightest minds in international politics predicted that Europe would once again become an incubator for world war. Articles in scholarly journals predicted that a resurgent and reunified Germany would burst through its borders and attack Poland, Czechoslovakia or Austria; that an ethnic conflict would erupt between Hungary and Romania; and that there would be a new arms race between Germany and Russia.[5] Instead, what happened was the least likely of all possible outcomes: Central and Eastern Europe were transformed into peaceful liberal democracies and were invited to join the European Union less than fifteen years after the fall of Communism. So how did Europe pull off this miracle in international relations?

As Robert Cooper argues, it began by introducing a European brand of surveillance with the first inspections regimes in the former Soviet Union. The Treaty on Conventional Armed Forces in Europe (or CFE Treaty), which was signed in Paris on 19 November 1990, marked the end of the Cold War. It set equal limits for East and West on the armaments that would be needed for conducting surprise attacks or initiating large-scale offensive operations. By the end of the treaty's reduction period in 1995, the thirty states that had signed it had destroyed or converted 52,000 battle tanks, armoured combat vehicles, artillery pieces, combat aircraft and attack helicopters. This was verified in over four thousand intrusive on-site inspections of military installations.[6] During centuries of the Balance of Power, Europeans had relied on the spectacle of military invasions or on building up vast stockpiles of weapons to deter their enemies. And then a single treaty had replaced that history of spectacle with a new regime based on surveillance.

But what was most exciting was the way that the very act of watching over these weapons removed the participant's desire to use them.[7] By becoming involved in each other's affairs, Europe and the former Soviet bloc came to see each other as partners rather than enemies. The original goal of the treaty was to make the balance of power work more effectively by ensuring that it was based on perfect information: if the two blocs opened themselves up to inspections it would be possible to ensure that they were perfectly balanced – like weighing scales. By keeping the balance at a low level, both sides could stop investing their precious resources in building up enormous arsenals of weapons and focus instead on ensuring the welfare of their citizens. Two competing blocs were transformed into a single security community with a common interest in maintaining the system. And as the two blocs became one community, the balancing purpose of the system was rendered irrelevant. The CFE Treaty had unintended consequences that have revolutionized our understanding of the potential of power as surveillance.

The CFE Treaty differed from the Iraqi inspections because it was both voluntary and mutual – in other words, the surveillance would work both ways and be in the self-interest of both sides. It was about creating a mutually beneficial peace, so surveillance could be introduced without the spectacle of military power. Once the military impediments had been removed, the political transformation of the region became possible – with the extraordinary enlargement first of NATO and then above all of the European Union.

The European Union did not just throw open its doors and invite these countries to join. Instead it linked the carrot of EU membership with a programme of deep-rooted transformation for any country that wanted to join. At the Copenhagen Summit in 1993, a series of criteria was agreed that all countries would have to fulfil:

'Membership requires that the candidate country has achieved stability of institutions guaranteeing democracy, the rule of law, human rights and respect for and protection of minorities, the existence of a functioning market economy, as well as the capacity to cope with competitive pressure and market forces within the Union. Membership presupposes the candidate's ability to take on the obligations of membership, including adherence to the aims of political, economic and monetary union.'[8]

In other words, all the countries that wanted to join would have to swallow all 80,000 pages of European laws and adapt their own legislation to accommodate them. And rather than taking these countries at their word, an army of officials and monitors were sent out to work with all the candidates for membership to check that the criteria were actually implemented.

This was nothing less than rebuilding these countries from the bottom up – and that is why, once the countries have changed, they will be altered for ever. The European model is the political equivalent of the strategy of the Jesuits: if you change the country at the beginning, you have it for life.

The Law as a Foreign Policy Tool

Europeans understand that the key to their success is the fact that their surveillance is voluntary and mutual. This means that it can be exercised in a very economical way without a vast disciplinary machine to enforce it. The European Union has developed an army of inspectors to examine the rule of law, and the legitimacy of elections around the world. The reason that European countries are so concerned about defending international legal norms is that the basis of the EU itself is simply an international treaty. Europeans therefore believe that things should be done through international law, and that the law can be a powerful way of entrenching a peaceful and democratic order.

On one level this has led to the encouragement of other common markets in Africa, Asia and Latin America. As the EU develops in confidence and global ambition, it will seek to create regional communities of interest that guarantee their security through transparency and mutual surveillance. For example, at the beginning of the year 2000, the British Prime Minister managed to persuade President Mbecki of South Africa and President Obasanjo of Nigeria that mutual surveillance could do for Africa what it has done for Europe. Together they developed the 'New Partnership for African Development'. This was a deal by which African countries would pledge to improve their records on democracy and the rule of law in exchange for an increase in aid, massive debt reduction and an effort to open Western markets to African products. At the heart of the process is the idea of mutual surveillance. Speaking on the occasion of the launch of the process, President Obasanjo described the peer review mechanism as 'an effective learning process that will ultimately place the fortune of Africa in its own hands'.[9] The peer review plan is designed by African leaders to monitor each other's performance on human rights, corruption and democracy. Countries that perform well against these criteria will be recompensed by getting a disproportionate amount of aid, trade and debt reductions.

At the same time, the EU builds provisions about human rights, the sanctity of contracts, and European competition policy into all of its dealings with other countries. In order to comprehensively change the countries it comes into contact with, European diplomacy starts not with military strategy, but domestic politics. Europeans believe that the best way to win the war on terror, control the proliferation of weapons of mass destruction, or wipe out organized crime and drugs is to spread the international rule of law. By helping to transform weak or autocratic states into well-governed allies, Europeans hope to be able to defend themselves from the greatest threats to their security.

The Law as a Tool of Transformative Power

At the heart of Europe's strategy is a revolutionary theory of international relations. Many foreign policy experts argue that foreign and domestic policy are fundamentally different. Domestic policy, they say, is hierarchical. They argue that in domestic politics a centralized state makes the law and enforces it when it is broken. The classical definition of a state is a body with a monopoly on legitimate force.[10] Foreign policy, by contrast, is anarchic – there are many competing states with no overarching government or global policeman to keep the peace.

But Foucault shows us that this image of domestic politics is wrong. The real reason that societies do not collapse into chaos is that their citizens do not want them to. Order is not produced through hierarchy, but because a majority of people have a stake in preserving order. That is why people internalize the rules and police themselves. The key to order, therefore, is co-opting people – or countries, for that matter – to uphold the rules themselves, rather than coercing them into submission. The same is true of the global system. A country like Luxembourg obeys the law because it has a stake in the legal order being preserved rather than because it fears the onset of German, American or UN tanks. Of the 192 countries in the world, only a dozen are outlaws or rogue states, and the reason that the other 180 obey the law is not because they are afraid of retribution. The question that Saddam Hussein's Iraq posed is: how do you give outlaws a stake in the system too?

CHAPTER 4

The Revolutionary Power of Passive Aggression

Beware the fate of Tantalus. The Ancient king of Sipylus in Asia Minor upset the gods by serving his son up at a dinner party and was sentenced to a life of perpetual frustration. He was immersed up to his neck in water, but when he bent to drink it all drained away; luscious fruit hung on trees above him, but when he reached for it the winds blew the branches beyond his reach. The gods could have smitten him from the face of the earth, but they made him suffer more by dangling untold wealth in front of him and then preventing him from ever enjoying it.

This is how the European Union wields its power today.

The ancient kingdom of Sipylus is in modern-day Turkey, and Tantalus' successors in the Turkish government can recognize his plight. Turkey first applied to join the European Union in 1963, and for four decades it has had the prospect of membership dangled in front of it but then removed because of the failings of the Turkish government. Turkish human rights abuses, restrictions on press freedom, the persecution of minorities, and the backwardness of the Turkish economy have all provided European governments with reasons to withdraw the nectar of membership. However, in Turkey today the prospect of joining the European club has become a unifying national dream – uniting secularists and Islamists with Anatolians, Kurds, and Armenians – behind a project that promises all a better future.

Over the last few years, the Turkish Parliament has passed six packages of constitutional amendments designed to bring Turkey in line with European standards. When the Prime Minister, Recep Tayip Erdogan, talks to his colleagues in Brussels, he boasts of abolishing the death penalty, the army-dominated security courts, and curbs on free speech. He can talk of how he has brought military budgets under civilian control for the first time ever, and of his 'zero tolerance for torture' in Turkish prisons. He has secured the release of Kurdish activists from prison, and allowed Turkish State Television, TRT, to begin broadcasting programmes in Kurdish and other minority languages such as Bosnian and Arabic. He has abandoned thirty years of intransigence on the Cyprus question, and erased centuries of mutual suspicion between Greece and Turkey with skilful diplomacy – so much so that Turkey's fiercest rival in the past has been transformed into one of the leading supporters of Turkish membership of the EU.[1] This revolution has come about for one reason alone: the Turkish desire to join the European Union.

Passive Aggression

Europe's effect on Turkey is a dramatic illustration of the power of 'passive aggression'. Rather than relying on the threat of exercising its power to secure its interests, Europe relies on the threat of not using it – of withdrawing the hand of friendship, and the prospect of membership.[2] For countries such as Turkey, Serbia, or Bosnia, the only thing worse than having the bureaucracy of Brussels descend on your political system, insisting on changes, implementing regulations, instigating state privatizations and generally seeping into every crack of everyday political life, is to have its doors closed to you.

The contrast between how Europe and America have dealt with their neighbours tells a powerful story. The threats are similar – drug trafficking, large flows of migrants across leaky borders, networks of international crime – but the responses could not be more different. The United States has sent troops into its neighbours more than fifteen times over the last fifty years[3] but many of the countries around it have barely changed – limping from crisis to crisis and often sucking American troops back into their problems. Although the individual circumstances are different, the story of American failure in Colombia stands in stark contrast to Europe's success in Turkey or the Balkans.

America is heavily involved in Colombia. It has given $1.3 billion in 'emergency aid', three-quarters of which is military and police aid. The USA funds training for the Colombian government's armed forces, has provided 18 Black Hawk and 42 Huey helicopters,[4] and has also given the government intelligence and surveillance equipment necessary to target coca crops and guerrilla-held areas. This involvement is explicitly part of the war on drugs, and a large proportion of the non-military aid is spent on coca substitution programmes to try to remove the overwhelming incentive for Colombian peasant farmers to feed the demand for cocaine in North America and Europe. The money is part of a broader, $7.5 billion 'Plan Colombia',[5] which the US government hopes will be able to steer the country out of the painful blind alley that civil war and reliance on drug production have sent it down. Yet peace has been elusive.

The US involvement in 'Plan Colombia' provides a powerful illustration of some of the reasons why American foreign policy fails to change the status quo: it generally pursues short-term goals that are explicitly in its own interest – the reduction of drug trafficking, the stabilization of a friendly government – and it utilizes its considerable armed force to do so, either by lending it to local proxies or by exercising it itself in a military intervention.

The European response, on the other hand, has been to hold out the possibility of integration (into the EU and into NATO) to neighbouring countries and so attempt to bring them closer to the political norms and institutional practices of the EU. By holding out these rewards, the Europeans are effectively making their neighbours an offer they cannot refuse. But once their neighbours take them up on it, they become an asset to the Europeans. One of La Fontaine's fables neatly illustrates this point.[6]

There once was a farmer who had three lazy sons. While he and his wife worked day and night to tend their vineyards the sons refused to lift a finger. On his deathbed the farmer told them that he had buried a treasure in the vineyard. The sons dug up every inch of the vineyard trying to find the pot of gold. After many years of searching, they never found the spot where the treasure was hidden. However, all of their digging cultivated the ground in the vineyard. Soon the grapevines produced such abundant fruit that the three lazy sons grew wealthy, unwittingly, from their own hard work.

This parable goes a long way to explain the positive effect of the European Union. The pot of gold of membership is powerful enough to motivate countries to go through the painful processes of reform that they need in order to be prosperous and free. And once they are prosperous and free they become an asset to the European Union rather than a burden.

The Eurosphere

Passive aggression has become the pattern for EU engagement in the world. Russia has been encouraged to sign the Kyoto Protocol by making aid conditional on its ratification; the United States has been encouraged to involve the UN in Iraq by the Franco-German refusal to get involved; Iran has been encouraged to sign the IAEA protocol on nuclear proliferation by an EU threat not to expand trade with the Islamic republic. We saw in the last chapter how the 80,000 pages of laws the EU has developed since the Common Market was formed in 1957, influencing everything from genetic labelling to human rights, have allowed Europe to spread its legislation and values across the world – from Australia to Zambia. It does this by making access to its market conditional on compliance with its mores. The power of the EU market has not just allowed Europeans to force large countries like the USA to back down on unfair tariffs on steel and other products: it has also allowed the EU to set a standard in global regulation.

Thousands of companies around the world have chosen to adopt the standards of the European Union rather than their domestic ones, so that they can gain access to the European market. Even mighty American multinationals have been forced to follow European rather than American regulations in at least three spheres: mergers and acquisitions, GM foods, and data privacy. The threat of exclusion from the European market was enough to bring down the GE–Honeywell merger – the largest industrial merger ever, worth $42 billion. This was just one in a long list, including the failed Time Warner–EMI, Sprint–Worldcom, and MCI–Worldcom mergers. The hunger for access to the EU market has seen many US companies accept regulation that they have fought against at home. On GM foods, the US government was forced to adopt European standards in food labelling when it was lobbied by farmers whose beef was not allowed to be sold in the EU. Another example is data privacy, for which Europe has much more stringent regulations which it has imposed on US companies under the 'Safe Harbour' protocol.

But the next wave of European transformations is only just beginning. The European Union is starting to develop an enormous sphere of influence, extending way beyond its borders, that could be called the 'Eurosphere'. This belt of eighty countries covering the former Soviet Union, the Western Balkans, the Middle East, North Africa, and Sub-Saharan Africa accounts for 20 per cent of the world's population (see Appendix).[7]

The EU is their largest trading partner, largest source of international bank credit, largest source of foreign direct investment, and largest provider of development assistance. Many of these countries use the euro as an anchor for their exchange rate policies or use the euro as a parallel currency alongside their domestic currency.

Europe has used this dependence to sign agreements with each of these countries that bring them under the European legal and political umbrella.[8] These agreements, which strengthen trade integration, open up current and capital accounts, and facilitate direct investment, also lay down political standards on human rights, good governance, and co-operation on crime and immigration. What is more, all European aid, apart from emergency aid, has conditions attached to it – governing human rights, migration policy, security, and economic reform.

It is early days yet. So far the potential for 'passive aggression' is greater than its impact in practice. It works most effectively on countries that are friendly – such as the United States or Central and Eastern Europe – and has been less successful in transforming unfriendly countries. What Europe is trying to do is to develop tools of 'passive aggression' that work on countries that are not candidates for membership. I explore this in Chapter 8.

The Most Exclusive Club in the World

Groucho Marx famously said that he would not want to join a club that would have him as a member, and one of the reasons for the enduring magnetism of the European Union is that it is the most exclusive club of all.[9] Its rules set a gold standard. The removal of barriers to free trade in Europe has gone much further than in any other trading bloc. The environmental and social labour standards are higher than anyone else's. The economic rules that need to be obeyed by members of the eurozone are stricter than the rules applied by the Fed or the Japanese Central Bank. And, finally, the standards of democracy, human rights and the protection of minorities far outstrip the standards required to join any other organization. These rules are so stringent and well thought through that many have gone beyond their European vocation and become global standards. When a superpower offers benefits to other countries if they change their behaviour they are accused of imperialism. When a club asks others to abide by the same rules as its own members it is seen as principled: this is what makes the European Union so compelling.

Europe's transformative power comes from its ability to reward reformers and withhold benefits from laggards. But passive aggression does not work on countries that do not want to join the club of law-abiding states. Dealing with them may involve using force.

CHAPTER 5

The European Way of War[1]

The European dream almost died in a town called Srebrenica.

In July 1995, what was supposed to be a United Nations Safe Area became a mass grave. While the 'blue helmets' looked on powerlessly, the Bosnian Serb army staged a brutal takeover of the ancient spa town and, over a period of five days, they systematically isolated the Muslim inhabitants and murdered over seven thousand men and boys, piling their bodies up in fields, schools, and warehouses.[2]

Genocide had returned to Europe. The leaders of the different Yugoslav factions had embraced all the tactics that the European project had rejected: military force to make political gains, ethnic nationalism to define identity, and 'ethnic cleansing' as a route to self-determination. But when Europe's leaders reached for a response they found the cupboard bare.

Everything they tried was simply used against them. The European obsession with rules was cynically manipulated by the Serbs, who scrupulously avoided firing at any UN troops when they overran the town. This meant that, under the UN's rules of engagement, European soldiers were not authorized to shoot at the Serbs, or respond with air strikes. The same thing happened with Europe's proposed peace settlements. Each time one was agreed, the Serbs used it as a means toward a military end rather than a stepping-stone to peace. They exposed the emptiness of a negotiated settlement that lacked the willingness to use force to back it up, dealing a critical blow to a European project committed to ending conflict by binding countries into a constant, unending process of negotiation. And even after peace was secured with American force, the former combatants thumbed their noses at the UN war crimes tribunal in The Hague by allowing wanted war criminals to live quite openly in the only country in the world, Bosnia, that was actually under the direct control of the UN itself.

The shame of Srebrenica still lives with us today. But that shame has driven Europe's leaders to develop a 'European Way of War'. Less than five years after the baleful response to the Bosnian crisis, a new generation of leaders – Tony Blair, Jacques Chirac, and, most remarkably since they had to change the German constitution to countenance it, Gerhard Schroeder and Joshka Fischer – were prepared to intervene in Kosovo. They were not just ready to go in, like the Americans, but some were even willing to countenance ground forces to back NATO's threats with credible force, unlike the Americans; and, furthermore, to do it without an explicit mandate from the United Nations. Three years after that, Europe's leaders agreed to intervene in Macedonia *before* the country descended into chaos.

But the European strategic doctrine is very different from America's. Military force is about building peace, not projecting power. Force may be necessary to defend Europe's values, but it will never be the heart of European foreign policy. Soldiers are deployed not to control other countries, but to remove the circumstances that led to war in the first place. European military action is above all about changing the fabric of a war-torn society. It is, in fact, about the spread of peace.

From Pacifism to Peace-Making

Europe's unwillingness to use force was different from America's famous casualty aversion. In fact, from the beginning of the crisis in Yugoslavia, European troops were put in harm's way, albeit in small numbers. Risks were taken to provide the humanitarian aid the UN sought to bring to its safe areas, and soldiers from many European countries died whilst operating under the UN mandate. But they were not allowed to fight. What stopped them was not just a fear of returning body bags and of Vietnamese-style quagmires, but an almost ideological aversion to conflict.

It was this that led them to impose the controversial arms embargo on all the factions in Yugoslavia, starving the Bosnian government of much-needed weaponry while leaving the Belgrade-backed Bosnian Serbs in firm control of the military balance, for fear of creating what Douglas Hurd shamefully referred to as a 'level killing field'.[3] It was also this that lay at the root of their opposition to American air strikes. Europeans did not just fear for their own troops in combat: they wanted no fighting of any kind. This was not cowardice, but pacifism.

Europe is the centre of an emerging tradition of thinking about international relations that the eminent military historian Michael Howard has called 'the Invention of Peace'. Howard quotes the nineteenth-century jurist Henry Maine, as saying: 'War appears to be as old as mankind, but peace is a modern invention.'[4] The idea of peace is distinct from what might be called 'negative peace' – merely the absence of war – and also from a Hobbesian definition of peace as a period where war is not actually, at that moment, being fought or prepared but will in due course occur again. The idea of an active, constructive international order of peace received its classic exposition in Kant's famous *Essay on Perpetual Peace*, which imagined a brotherhood of republics which, because they reflected the wishes of their peoples, would never countenance war against each other. It was towards this system of international relations that Europeans had been working, more or less consciously, since 1945, and European pacifism in the face of the belligerence of a Milosevic was in part the result of a reluctance to admit that this utopia had not been achieved.

The Balkans, therefore, represented a new kind of asymmetrical warfare, not of assets, but of values. The Serbs did not outmanoeuvre their opponents by winning on the battlefield, but they took advantage of their attachment to the value of compromise. The Europeans had ignored Karl von Clausewitz's famous argument on the inevitability of warfare. When one party is prepared to use extreme measures in a dispute, he argued, the other party must follow suit or else capitulate.[5] The Europeans thought that negotiated settlements would hold themselves up without the backing of force. But in Bosnia, Serb and Croat nationalists were guided by an absolutist politics of tribalism rather than the politics of negotiation and compromise that reigned within the rest of Europe.

After the horror of Bosnia, a new generation of European leaders was determined to back up law with force. This shift in mood paved the way for three new strands in European thinking on the use of force that sought to remedy the defects of European power so cruelly exposed in the early 1990s: humanitarian intervention, a European doctrine of pre-emption, and state-building.

From Pacifism to Humanitarian Intervention

In the middle of the Kosovo crisis in 1999, the British Prime Minister Tony Blair travelled to America to shore up President Clinton's resolve to stay the course. In a now famous speech to the Chicago Press Club, he first set out the doctrine of 'humanitarian intervention'. Humanitarian intervention was an answer to the difficulties with humanitarian pacifism that events like the fall of Srebrenica had exposed.[6]

By intervening in Kosovo, Europeans put military intervention back into a continuum of engagement that spanned diplomatic support, aid, governance assistance, and sanctions. They have made an impressive shift in this direction, quietly doubling the numbers of troops posted overseas over the last decade.

The average number of European troops deployed outside the EU and NATO areas was 70,000 during 2003 – peaking at 90,000 during the British deployment to Iraq. These were spread over twenty countries in South-East Europe, Afghanistan and Central Asia, in Iraq and the Gulf, and in Africa.[7] In 2003, the EU also launched its first long-range operation, 'Operation Artemis', in the Eastern Congo, responding to a request from the UN Secretary-General by deploying 1,400 troops, at seven days' notice, to Bunia to stabilize the region while the slower process of assembling a UN peace-keeping force got under way.[8] These troops are not settled in bases around the world to defend pipelines, economic interests, or the balance of power. Instead they are almost all operating under the flag of the United Nations to support humanitarian goals.

The European Security Strategy which was signed in December 2003 shows that Europeans are already preparing for the next set of challenges, as enlargement brings the European Union closer to the 'arc of instability' on its southern and eastern flanks, stretching from Agadir on the Atlantic to Astrakhan on the Caspian Sea.[9] When Romania, Bulgaria, the Western Balkans and Turkey join, Europe will need to be ready to deal with neighbours that include Iran, Iraq, Georgia, Moldova, and Belarus.

Preventive Engagement

After the debacle in the Balkans, Europe's leaders agreed a new strategic imperative: act early. The goal is to employ European power while it still has the opportunity of working, before the idea of political compromise is made impossible, and to ensure the presence of a credible threat of force, in order to make that compromise stick. This is summed up in the European Security Strategy's talk of 'preventive engagement', a European answer to the Bush doctrine of 'preventive war'.

The contrast between the two doctrines is stark. The Bush doctrine attempts to justify action to remove a 'threat' before it has the chance of being employed against the United States. It is consequently focused very closely on physical assets and capabilities, necessarily swift in execution and therefore short-term in conception, and unavoidably entirely military in kind. The European doctrine of pre-emption, in contrast, is predicated on a long-term involvement, with the military just one strand of activity, along with pre-emptive economic and legal intervention, and is aimed at building the political and institutional bases of stability, rather than simply removing the immediate source of threat.

Preventive engagement is an attempt to ward off the dangers of European autism. In the past, Europe has been so wrapped up in building its single currency and changing its institutions that it has allowed its neighbourhood to collapse into chaos. Europe's leaders now realize that the European Union cannot be prosperous if its neighbourhood is a hotbed of war and ethnic violence. Now, the imperative is to get in early, as in Macedonia ('Operation Concordia') in 2003, with troops, negotiations, and institution-building, to separate the warring factions, disarm the paramilitaries and prevent an ethnic nationalist war from taking root. Acting pre-emptively before threats arise is not simply more effective, but also a lot less costly. The contrast between the slow and disastrous reaction to Bosnia, the faster and more determined action in Kosovo, and an intervention before things descended into chaos in Macedonia was dramatic in terms of loss of life. The difference in financial costs is equally striking: the failure in Bosnia cost the British taxpayer at least £1.5 billion. Kosovo cost £200 million. Macedonia cost just £14 million.[10]

Engagement Strategies, Not Exit Strategies

Europeans will rarely consider using force without planning how to put things back together again afterwards. While most American policy makers talk about 'nation-building', the Europeans have a different approach that could be called state-building. The lessons from Bosnia, Iraq, Afghanistan and many African countries are that the challenge is not building 'nations', but building 'states', very often in areas where several nations and nationalities have to coexist within a single state. In the Balkans, the need is to create political structures that contain and challenge ethnic nationalism rather than adding fuel to it.[11]

For Europeans, the goal is not to get in and out as quickly as possible. It is to bring about the transformation of the country, and if it is in Europe, set it on course to eventually join the European Union. The international protectorate in Bosnia has already lasted longer than the full-scale allied military occupation of Germany after 1945. It is still far from being self-sustaining. The core functions of state-building in Bosnia have been consciously designed to feed into the process of EU accession: building institutions, establishing the rule of law and economic reform, as well as encouraging refugees to return.

After the fighting subsided, the EU quickly negotiated a series of unilateral trade concessions with the Balkan countries that led on to 'Stabilization and Association Agreements'. Again, these programmes started to shape the legal structure and political architecture of these countries in line with the *acquis communautaire*. This was formalized in 2002, when Paddy Ashdown, as the UN High Representative, also became the EU's envoy to Bosnia, thereby clearing a path for eventual membership of the European Union.

Europe's new state-building is an application of European incentives alongside hard military and political power. It is hard work, as the precarious status of Kosovo proves. But by using force to establish security on the ground, the EU has found that its original aim of smothering the conflict with promises of EU accession and institutionalized negotiation is more likely to succeed.

Escaping from the Shadow of American Military Doctrine

The common theme that drives American discussion of Europe's security strategy is despair about Europe's lack of capacity and the unwillingness of European governments to spend as much on defence as the Americans. But the problem is not really spending: the twenty-five EU governments spend approximately 180 billion a year on defence, which is second only to the Americans 330 billion. But, as many have noted, Europeans only get a fraction of the bang for their buck as the Americans. While the USA can send about 400,000 ground troops around the world out of a total of 650,000, the EU can deploy barely 85,000 out of a total of 1.2 million ground soldiers. And when it comes to satellite intelligence, transport aircraft, battle-carriers and precision-guided missiles, Europeans are miles behind.[12]

But these constant comparisons with America are not helpful because Europe will never need to fight against the American military machine. Europeans can build peace through military interventions without mimicking the American way of war.

It is true that European governments did not have the planes, intelligence and precision weapons to fight the war in Kosovo like the Americans. But they could have fought that war differently, with a greater stress from the start on preparations for a land war. Lawrence Freedman compares the plight of the Iranians in the 1980s who spent six years outside Basra, unable to make headway against Iraqi defences, with the British campaign in 2003 which took exactly eight days.[13] This shows that European troops are more than capable of taking on their most likely opponents. In fact, in many types of fighting, the European way of war might actually be more appropriate than the American way. The Kosovo campaign showed that a war fought from 15,000 feet in the air is highly inefficient. The bombing campaign accelerated the humanitarian crisis and was not geared to dealing with guerrilla fighters in the hills. Many commentators have pointed out that the American military doctrine is dysfunctional – preparing the military for fights against big threats at a time when most wars are small and unconventional.[14]

In the Balkans, Somalia, Afghanistan, Iraq or Chechnya, war is not against national armies with battleships, planes and tanks. Instead, it is about fighting street by street, and house by house, against local insurgents. You need to be able to occupy and control territory in the face of a hostile local population. As Anatole Lieven points out, the challenge in these situations is not more firepower, but less. In fact, the American obsession with firepower and force protection is likely to lead to an unacceptable level of civilian casualties.[15]

The differences between the European approach and that of the Americans came out in Iraq. In Baghdad, the American counter-insurgency operation mobilized the whole civilian population against the occupation, while the British approach in Basra was driven by an attempt to separate the insurgents from the local population. Europeans are better at this than the Americans because their main military experience is peace-keeping and imperial policing, rather than conventional warfare.[16]

Europeans urgently need to invest in their capabilities – but they should do so on their own terms. Recent summits have agreed to establish 'Battle Groups' that can be deployed within days to stabilize civil wars; a Rapid Reaction Force of 60,000 deployable in sixty days; a European Foreign Minister to co-ordinate different policies; a European Security Strategy; and a European Defence Capabilities Agency. The American defence expert Michael O'Hanlon is optimistic that, with very little extra spending, Europeans could significantly enhance their capabilities. By diverting just 10 per cent of their defence budgets to buy specific types of equipment – such as long-range transport planes and ships, unmanned aerial vehicles and precision-guided missiles – within a decade, they could deploy 200,000 high-quality, professional soldiers anywhere in the world. Cutting manpower by a quarter and focusing on developing highly trained combat troops would pay for this.[17] This is the direction in which Europeans are slowly moving.

Europeans have learned the hard way that to promote peace you sometimes need to go to war. But even with the development of European military capabilities, Europeans will rely less on the use of force to shape the world than any other major power. What makes the European Union unique is that it can bring together its aid, trade and development assistance to prevent hotspots from collapsing into war.[18] Its forces do not just include fighters, but an army of 45,000 diplomats, 5,000 police, 2,000 aid-workers for disaster relief, as well as pools of magistrates and election monitors.[19]

The first four chapters of this book have shown how the lack of a military option has led the European Union to develop creative ways of shaping the world around it by deploying its body of law, and then backing it up with the might of its market. The real success of European foreign policy will still be to avoid fighting at all.

CHAPTER 6

The Stockholm Consensus

'Porridge together is better than pork cutlets alone.' This is the philosophy of the residents of a Stockholm commune who have opted out of the rat race to pursue a life of simple pleasure. These bearded, long-haired idealists share everything: their bodies (open relationships, experiments with lesbianism, 'airing' their vaginas in the kitchen), their possessions (Abba LPs, root vegetables, a battered Volkswagen van), their leisure time (the children's favourite game is playing 'Pinochet' by taking it in turns to torture and be tortured), and their conflicting interpretations of Marxist-Leninist thought (the biggest debate is whether or not washing up is bourgeois).[1] But Erik, Gustav, and Lena, whose communal life is depicted in Lukas Moodysson's gentle film *Together*, are gradually forced to give up on their idealism. The arrival of newcomers and the ravenous demands for consumerism of the younger generation erode the community's values: the vegetarianism is relaxed, the ban on television eased, and eventually each of the inhabitants abandons communal life in favour of material wealth. Is this a metaphor for the European Union, whose attempts to create a paradise on earth for the existing generation are being threatened by globalization, a demographic time bomb, and sluggish economic growth?

Many Americans see the European economy as the business equivalent of a hippy commune – mired in the 1970s, unable to reform because of the cacophony of voices that erupt every time a decision needs to be made, and more interested in soft-headed ideas of quality of life than economic performance. They argue that it will not succeed until it emulates the USA with lower taxes, less social protection, a smaller state, and a narrow focus on shareholder value.

There is just one problem with this conventional wisdom – it is not supported by the facts. Sweden is no longer the country of Björn Borg, Abba, Pippi Longstocking, bad porn movies, and worse haircuts. Its new economic icons are world-beating companies like Ikea, Ericsson, Volvo, Saab, Absolut Vodka, Astra Zeneca, and Hennes & Mauritz. Its vital statistics are the envy of the world, with 75 per cent of the population in employment and steady growth through the 1990s.[2] But, unlike America, it continues to have low levels of inequality, high tax levels, strong trade unions, and a large public sector.

Sweden is not alone: many European countries have outperformed the USA on a whole series of indicators ranging from competitiveness and employment to R&D and innovation. In just ten years Finland has moved from being a sleepy agricultural backwater – dependent on the Soviet Union for most of its markets – to leading the world in IT and mobile phones (with Nokia making up over 30 per cent of the global mobile phones market, and Linux as the only real global challenger to Microsoft).[3] Ireland has gone through a similar process, leaving its agricultural past behind to become the Celtic Tiger. Holland and Denmark have had some of the best job-creation records over the last decade through the growth of part-time jobs in the service sector, higher female employment, and wage moderation. These are the economies that are already being copied by other Europeans: Germany has developed its Agenda 2010 proposals, France has launched an ambitious programme of structural reforms, while the new members from Poland to Estonia have modernized their economies at a startling pace.[4]

Europe's transformative power could one day spread to the economic world. As large countries like Brazil, South Africa, India and China develop, they would do well to examine a unique economic model that combines the economies of scale of a continental market with high levels of productivity to deliver the security and equality that come from strong national welfare states.

Europe's Economic Growth

Europe's added value comes from the quality of life it delivers rather than its growth rates, but even on the traditional metrics of economic performance, Europe's record is far more respectable than its American critics imply.

For the individual worker in Europe, wages have grown more than for his or her counterpart in the United States – even during the miracle decade of the 1990s. GDP per head has risen at almost the same level in Europe and America, but Americans have had to work longer hours and take shorter holidays to keep up with their European counterparts. Some commentators have even gone as far as to say that the real story of the last ten years is less one of an American economic miracle than one of American underperformance.[5]

In fact, many Americans have seen their wages fall even as their economy has grown. Real earnings of production workers dropped by 14 per cent in the private sector from 1973 to 1995. After a 5 per cent increase between 1995 and 1999, they trailed off again after the recession of 2001. The official Census Bureau figures show that between 2001 and 2004 the annual income of the average family fell by $1,511.[6] This exposes the problem with one of the most over-cited figures in the economic world: that America's GDP grew at an average of 3 per cent a year in the ten years to 2003 – compared to just 1.8 per cent in the eurozone.[7]

The truth is that this overall figure hides the fact that the growth in the US economy has been driven by a growing population rather than better economic performance. Population growth in the USA in the 1990s averaged 1.2 per cent a year compared with 0.5 per cent a year in the eurozone. This means that if you look at the average GDP per person, the US growth collapses to 2.1 per cent, narrowing the gap between the two continents to just 0.3 per cent. What is more, the EU's underperformance can be explained by a single country, Germany, which has been struggling with the costs of re-unification. This may be cheating, but if you take Germany out of the calculations, the gap between Europe and America actually disappears, leaving Europe and the USA with identical figures.[8]

Another misapprehension is that America's productivity is racing ahead of the eurozone's. Kevin Daly of Goldman Sachs argues that the level of eurozone productivity, when defined as output per hour, was only 4 per cent less than the USA's in 2003, slightly better than the position ten years ago[9] (much of this can be explained by geography, as the retail sector in America is based around out-of-town strip malls while many of the EU's shops are on the high street).[10] The reason that Americans have a greater overall output than Europeans is simple: Americans work longer hours. By 2003, annual hours worked per capita in the USA were 866 compared to 691 in the EU-15.[11] Much of this difference is due to the fact that the average US worker takes only ten days' holiday each year. In contrast, in several European countries workers average thirty days or more.[12]

Perhaps the most widespread myth is that America's rise in productivity has created jobs while Europe's has destroyed them: over the past decade total employment in the USA has expanded by 1.3 per cent a year compared to just 1 per cent in the eurozone. However, after the exclusion of Germany, the performances of the USA and the eurozone are indistinguishable over the decade, while since 1997 the eurozone has performed better (total employment rose by 8 per cent compared to America's 6 per cent). And even that 6 per cent figure is misleading, according to an official US report, because it doesn't account for the fact that almost 1 per cent of the US population is in prison.[13] It is true that European countries fall far behind on the employment of over-55s and women, but as we will see later, several European governments have bucked the trend of early retirement and developed policies to entice mothers back into the workplace.

Above all these figures give the lie to the idea that there is a crude trade-off between employment and equality – that the only route to high employment is one of bad jobs, high insecurity, poverty pay and extreme inequalities. On the contrary, it is the countries with the most generous welfare states – Sweden, Denmark, Norway, Ireland and the Netherlands – that have the highest levels of total employment. Each one of these countries comfortably outperforms the United States. The UK, Finland, Portugal, and Austria are all on their way to catching up with the USA[14] with participation rates around the 70 per cent mark. The reason for this is that they have shifted from having passive welfare states that provide a safety net for the sick to active ones that turn the State into a motor of opportunity.

The final misapprehension is that Europe's companies are underperforming because they balance their commitment to shareholder value with responsibilities to their staff and the wider community. Many of the biggest companies in the world are in fact European: 61 of the 140 biggest companies on the Global Fortune 500 rankings come from Europe (compared to 50 from the USA and 29 from Asia).[15] And in key sectors – energy, telecoms, aeroplanes, commercial banking, and pharmaceuticals – it is European companies that are setting the pace for global business. The remarkable stories of Vodafone, which is the largest wireless player in the world, and the Airbus consortium, which brought together European companies to comprehensively outperform the American Boeing Company, show that in many of the sectors of the future, the American board room is trailing Europe's lead.[16]

Defusing the Demographic Time Bomb

The most powerful argument for euro-pessimism is Europe's falling birth rate. The nightmare scenario is of the European economy being gradually hollowed out as a bloated population of pensioners lives off the backs of an ever smaller pool of workers. Over-60s, as a proportion of the population of conventional working age, have increased from 20 per cent in 1960 to 35 per cent in 2000. The figure is forecast to grow to 47 per cent in 2020 and 70 per cent in 2050, leading to a European Commission forecast that annual growth could decline from around 2 per cent to 1¼ per cent by 2040.[17]

But the fact that demographers have spotted a trend does not mean that it will lead inexorably to disaster: most demographic predictions – dating right back to Thomas Malthus and his apocalyptic visions of the rise in population leading to mass starvation – have been wrong. And there are many signs that today's merchants of doom will be mistaken. After years of a falling birth rate, Sweden, Denmark, Norway, Britain, and France are showing signs of a reverse while others are learning from their example. Italy, Germany, and Spain (three of the countries with the lowest birth rates) are now introducing financial and fiscal incentives to couples to produce more children. And as the Scandinavian and French examples show, the provision of adequate maternity (and paternity) rights and childcare facilities can have an even more dramatic effect than financial or fiscal incentives.

The pensions debate has also become misleading. Every study has shown that the simple move of raising the retiring age can immediately remove the ticking time bomb of growing dependency ratios.[18] The European Commission forecasts that if member-states succeed in raising the average retirement age by five years from sixty to sixty-five, without raising benefits, the cost of Europe's pension system would remain stable.[19] This is a painful political challenge, but it is one that all European governments are already grappling with, through pension reforms – many based on a Swedish template – that will reduce the fiscal pressures from population ageing and encourage longer working lives.

Another partial solution to Europe's demographic dilemma is the move towards supporting 'managed migration' that has taken hold across Europe. All European countries are now ending their blanket ban on economic migration and developing criteria for admitting labour migrants based on qualifications or salary. Unskilled labour will be admitted according to seasonal need, when shortages can be acute, thereby avoiding incentives for illegal trafficking.

What is more, it is not just Europe that faces this problem. Academics show us that once the economy develops, literacy rates improve, women become empowered and then fertility drops. Thus Chinese growth could be undermined by its age-ing population. In the USA the problem is currently mitigated by a higher birth rate and immigration, but it is questionable whether the latter can continue forever (not least in the current geo-political climate). The key is to find ways to stabilize dependency ratios. Europe is one of the first con-tinents to grapple with these issues, and has already had some success in offsetting the problem.

The Euro and the Dollar

There are three reasons why the European project should make us more optimistic about the European economy in the future.

The first is the euro, which could allow the EU to accrue some of the benefits that the dollar's pre-eminence has afforded the United States. In many ways, the dollar is the dirty secret behind the US economic miracle, allowing the lonely superpower to finance its own balance of payments deficit by selling foreigners a currency that is depreciating in value. But there are reasons to doubt that the rest of the world will tolerate America's profligacy indefinitely. America has a current account deficit of 5 per cent of GDP while the euro area has a surplus. American households now save less than 2 per cent of GDP compared to 12 per cent in the eurozone, and total household debt stands at 84 per cent of GDP (compared to 50 per cent in the eurozone). This is not sustainable – as the economist Herb Stein has argued, 'things which can't go on forever usually don't'.

Although the US dollar still accounts for approximately two thirds of all official currency reserves, there is a definite trend away from it and towards the euro. Several countries have already converted some or all of their reserves into euros. At the moment, the euro only makes up 18.7 per cent of official global foreign exchange reserves, to the dollar's 64.5 per cent, but the trend is that the euro is making up an ever increasing share. There are approximately 150 countries in the world that have exchange rate regimes tied to an anchor or reference currency: 51 currently use the euro, or have the euro as a major part of their reference basket.[20]

These still make up a small percentage of the world's currencies, but the shift to the euro is accelerating: Russia increased its euro reserves in 2003 to approximately 25 per cent of its total reserve of $65 billion, and China has also recognized the growing importance of the euro as a reserve currency. Towards the end of 2003 rumours were circulating that the OPEC countries were considering switching the pricing of oil into euros, since the continued weakness of the dollar was substantially hurting their revenues and forcing them to increase production. Such a switch in currency pricing for the world's largest physical commodity (12 per cent of world trade) would contribute significantly in raising the euro's status to that of the world's leading international currency through its increased use as a medium of exchange. The big change will occur when Asian central bankers shift some of their reserves into euros, something which is very much on their agenda according to an executive at a City institution whose clients include several Asian central banks. Romano Prodi told me that when he first met the Chinese President Jiang Zemin, his Chinese interlocutor was fascinated by the euro. Apparently, his parting words were: 'We will switch our reserves to the euro for two reasons. Why? First because we believe in multipolarity. Second, because it will be good business.'

If the euro emerges as a global reserve currency, it will give the countries of the Eurozone much greater control over their economic futures. Europe will probably not mimic the American model of using its status as one of the world's bankers to finance a huge current account deficit, but a massive injection of capital into the European economy would undoubtedly stimulate demand.

As the Nobel Prize-winner Robert Mundell argues: 'The advent of the euro may turn out to be the most important development in international monetary arrangements since the emergence of the dollar as the dominant currency shortly after the creation of the US central bank, the Federal Reserve System, in 1913 ... the euro area could easily contain as many as 50 countries with a population exceeding 500 million and a GDP substantially larger than the United States within a decade.'

The Continent of Energy Independence

The second reason to be optimistic about Europe's economy is energy. The European Union is far ahead of America and Asia in the race to end its dependence on natural resources – to make it the first continent of 'energy independence'. It understands that preserving the planet for future generations is not just an existential challenge, it also makes good economic sense.

North America is already the largest consumer of oil in the world, accounting for more than a quarter of total demand in 2001. What is more, oil demand in the USA is projected to grow by 1.7 per cent per year. Most of the growth is projected for the transportation sector, with cars and light truck fleets – including sport utility vehicles (SUVs) – being the largest consuming segment of the sector.

Europe, on the other hand, has been leading the world in

the shift to renewable sources of energy. It already accounts for only 3,176 million tonnes of CO_2 emissions compared to America's 6,016 million tonnes. This means that <u>every American citizen causes three times as many CO_2 emissions as a European</u>. From January 2005, the European Union hopes to have in place the world's biggest and most effective emissions trading scheme, covering over 12,000 energy-producing and energy-intensive plants across the EU. The scheme will offer businesses a cost-effective way of both reducing their emissions and covering the bill for action to help prevent climate change.

And many countries are well on the way to kicking the carbon habit. In Sweden, for example, <u>only 40 per cent of energy comes from oil</u>, with 40 per cent coming from renewable sources and 20 per cent from nuclear power. In 2000, Sweden introduced the 'green tax shift' which saw the country shift tax away from labour and towards energy consumption over a ten-year period. The government has also issued 'green certificates' to stimulate production of 'bioenergy', wind power and solar energy.[21]

There is talk of adopting this certification system at the European level. The recent past has already seen a surge in oil prices that could cripple the US economy and seriously hold back the development of China and India, and the future is likely to be even worse. Analysts estimate that between 2000 and 2020 China's energy consumption will rise by 3.8 per cent a year; while US consumption will go up by 1.4 per cent per year. With its current low levels of consumption, and increases predicted at a modest 0.7 per cent per year, Europe may soon reap the rewards of its 'energy independence'.[22]

The Power of Integration and Enlargement

Possibly the biggest boon to European economies is the European project itself. Europe's economic strength rests on two pillars: the overall size of its economy which assures it power in the world, and the quality of living standards it can deliver for its citizens. Both have been improved by the continuing integration and enlargement of the European Union.

The impact of the creation of the Single Market in 1992 has already been dramatic. The European Commission estimates that European Union's GDP in 2002 was almost 2 per cent higher than it would have been without the creation of the internal market, while employment was almost 1.5 per cent higher. The single market has also led to a doubling of Foreign Direct Investment in the EU, and the competition has forced prices for consumers down to record levels (with air prices falling by over 40% and phone prices by over half).[23]

The impact of enlargement could be equally transformative. The European Commission estimates that the fact of enlargement alone will increase the GDP growth of the new members by between 1.3 and 2.1 percentage points every year, while enlargement will add an extra 0.7 per cent a year to the existing members' growth rates.[24]

A study by Goldman Sachs argues that within half a century, the Chinese, Indian, Brazilian, and Russian economies will be bigger than any of the European economies in the G7 (America, Japan, Germany, France, Britain, Italy, and Canada). Today, their combined GDP (at market exchange rates) is one-eighth of the output of the G6.[25] But the study concludes that the total output of the four economies will overtake that of the G7 in less than forty years.[26]

This has led to predictions of Europe's economic irrelevance in the twenty-first century. But the report simply shows how misleading it is to extrapolate the economic future without taking European integration into account. Europe's strength in the world comes from the collective weight of the European economy (which will continue to grow as the EU enlarges) rather than the size of its component economies. The reason that Germany, France, and Britain can negotiate trade as equals with the United States is not because they are in the G7 but because they are in the European Union. It is possible that the relative size of each of these countries' economies will be smaller in 2050 than it is today, but it is likely that the European Union as a bloc will be even bigger as the Union grows to absorb its neighbouring countries.

If the ten new members close the gap between their standard of living and the Western European one, in the same way that Ireland, Spain, and Portugal did after they joined, it will have a massive tonic effect on the European economy. A study by Lehman Brothers argues that such a growth in the economies of the accession countries could lead to a scenario where 'notwithstanding its ageing population, with the right policies, Europe could actually see its weight in the world economy increase over the next 15 years. By 2020, the EU could have a lead over the US of about 45%.' And a Europe with fifty members will be an even more serious economic player than the Euro-25.[27]

The Stockholm Consensus vs. the American Business Model

But the success of an economic model goes beyond the size of GDP: it depends on its ability to attract others and through that to set the rules for the global economy.

The real costs of the American economic model are becoming ever clearer. Professor Robert Gordon of Northwestern University shows that the size of the American GDP hides the fact that much of it is going into unproductive things:

- Cars rather than public transport: for example, Americans must buy cars because public transport is so lousy. The value of the cars is calculated in American GDP, but European public-transport systems are counted not at their value to passengers but as a cost to government.

- The social costs of inequality. For example, Americans keep two million of their fellow citizens in jail: the cost of building the prisons and paying the jailers is also included in GDP.

- Air conditioning and heating. America's more extreme climate – colder winters (save in Florida and California) and hotter summers (save in Washington, Oregon, and California) – means it must spend more on heating and cooling.

If you add all these 'sunk costs' into the mix, Gordon argues that although Western Europeans only work three-quarters as much as Americans, they get ninety per cent of the return, coupled with far more equal income distributions and lower poverty rates.[28] In the future, Europe might not keep up with the voracious consumption of an American economy that puts growth above all else, but the European economic model is robust enough to pay for a quality of life for European citizens that is among the best in the world.

All European countries today are reforming their economies for an age of economic interdependence, while trying to keep the best features of the European social model intact. They could be said to converging around a 'Stockholm Consensus', as the Swedish state has pioneered so many of these new approaches. The 'Stockholm Consensus' amounts to nothing less than a new social contract in which a strong and flexible state underpins an innovative, open, knowledge economy. This contract means that the state provides the resources for educating its citizens, treating their illnesses, providing childcare so they can work, and integration lessons for newcomers. In exchange, citizens take training, are more flexible, and newcomers integrate themselves.

The 'Stockholm Consensus' stands in opposition to much of the waste of the 'Washington Consensus': low levels of inequality allow Europeans to save on crime and prison; energy-efficient economies protect them from hikes in oil prices; the social contract gives people leisure and a helping hand back into work if they lose their jobs; while the European single market and the euro will allow European countries to benefit from economies of scale in a global market without giving up on the adaptability and dynamism that come from being small.

In many parts of the world – from Beijing to Brasilia –

countries that have been through periods of rapid economic growth are now focusing on how to deliver a better quality of life for those at the bottom of the pyramid. The sociologist Amitai Etzioni offers a cultural explanation for this resistance to the American business model in many parts of the world: 'While the Western position is centred around the individual, the focus of Eastern cultures tends to be towards a strongly ✗ ordered community.'

In other words, if the United States represents the ultimate symbol of a rights-based culture and a focus on individual wealth, Asia is more interested in the idea of 'responsibility' and the creation of common good. Europe, through the 'Stockholm Consensus', can offer the best of both worlds; a synthesis of the dynamism of liberalism with the stability and welfare of social democracy. As the world becomes richer and moves beyond satisfying basic needs such as hunger and health, the European way of life will become irresistible.

CHAPTER 7

The European Rescue of National Democracy[1]

If there is one image that symbolizes democracy around the world, it was the sight of East German students clambering onto the Berlin wall on 9 November 1989, hacking it to pieces with pickaxes as the soldiers looked on in awe. Within two years these students were citizens of the European Union in a reunited Germany. The EU sucked in the former communist republics, bringing democracy and prosperity in its wake.

And yet today, many accuse the European Union of destroying our democracy even as it spreads it across the Continent. They accuse it of devouring our national political systems and putting decisions in the hands of bureaucrats in Brussels. They argue that the European Commission is an unelected technocracy, that the European Council of Ministers meets behind closed doors, and that the only directly elected institution, the European Parliament, has failed to inspire European citizens.[2]

Listening to this rhetoric, you could be forgiven for thinking that the bureaucrats in Brussels are free to wield their power like modern-day monarchs – corrupt, making arbitrary decisions, and out of control. But what is striking about the EU, to anyone who studies it, is not how much power it wields, but how weak its decision-making powers are. It doesn't set levels of tax, provide healthcare, pensions, unemployment benefits, oversee a police force, or command an army. The treaties only allow it to make policy in areas that cut across borders; so its focus is mainly on regulating the single market, protecting the environment, delivering foreign aid, regulating interest rates, and co-ordinating foreign and defence policies.[3]

It is true that the European Commission proposes legislation, but the decisions are all taken by national governments. In many policy areas, decisions need to be agreed by unanimity, which means that any government can veto them. And even when decisions can be taken by majority voting, the winning side must gather between 74 and 100 per cent of the votes[4] – a higher threshold than any parliamentary system in the world. What's more, the twenty-five national parliaments hold their governments to account, and have some discretion on how to implement EU decisions. If that were not enough, there is also a directly elected European Parliament, the first multinational parliament in history, which must agree to all legislation that is decided by majority voting.

The European Parliament also has the power to sack or veto the European Commission, a power that shows the Commission is not unaccountable. In May 1999 they forced the Santer Commission to resign en masse because of mismanagement and accusations of fraud; and in October 2004 they forced Commission President Barroso to reshuffle his team of Commissioners because the conservative views of Rocco Buttiglione, the nominee for Justice Commissioner, on immigration, women's rights and sexual orientation made him the wrong person for the job.[5]

In his famous Gettysburg Address, Abraham Lincoln talked of democracy as 'government of the people, by the people for the people'. What he meant was that democracies exist to hold the state to account, and to make sure that the policies that are implemented correspond to what people want. Set against those tests, the EU fares pretty well. It is not about destroying democracy but reinventing it to empower governments and their citizens in an age of globalization.

How Europe Empowers Governments

One of Tony Blair's closest political advisers, Philip Gould, talks about politics becoming 'an empty stadium'.[6] Politicians continue to campaign, they publish manifestos, and they argue things out in the age-old ways. The big difference is that no one is listening. Voter turnout is falling, membership of political parties is in decline, and the trust that people place in politicians and political institutions has plummeted to dangerously low levels.

But why is the stadium empty? Is it because politicians are sleazier or less engaging than they were? Is it because people are wealthier and don't need politicians to provide them with the basic things – sanitation, food, or a job? Or is it because political parties struggle to represent citizens who no longer vote according to their social class? Maybe these are all part of the problem; but the one thing that all opinion polls point towards is that people don't think that politics can actually make a difference any more. All over the world, voters are turning away from national governments that they regard as powerless. They see them as plastic ducks bobbing in the choppy seas of global capitalism and American hegemony, and blaming global events for their failure to deliver on their promises.

Europe is seen as part of the problem, leaching away government power to institutions miles away in Brussels. But far from being part of the problem, the European Union is the remedy: giving countries control over policies that had become global.

Witness the tale of two northern European countries. Norway and Ireland have a population of around 4 million. Both export salmon and both do most of their trade with the European Union. One is in the European Union, the other is not. While Norway has had to adopt 80 per cent of EU legislation in order to join the European Economic Area,[7] it has had no say on its content, while Ireland has had a seat at the table from the beginning. While Norway must pay tariffs to export its smoked salmon to the rest of the EU, Irish farmers face no such costs. And when the World Trade Organization sets global trade rules for fisheries, the Irish perspective is represented by the European Commissioner, Peter Mandelson, as part of the bargaining position of the biggest single market in the world, while the Norwegian Trade Minister only has the clout of the world's 122nd biggest country behind his demands. And when it comes to dealing with pollution, organized crime and the flow of drugs, Ireland is able to use the European Union to demand tough measures from Russia, Poland or the Balkan countries, while Norway must depend on the goodwill of its eastern neighbours and the power of example.[8]

Who has more control over their affairs? The Irish have a vote and a veto in European discussions but they are then bound to abide by whatever Europe collectively decides. The Norwegians are not bound to abide by the decisions of the EU, in which they play no part, but if they reject them they will lose access to their biggest market. And when it comes to global negotiations, who has more power? The Irish can put forward their perspective and have it reflected in the EU's negotiating position. They will need to compromise with the other twenty-five member-states, but once they have persuaded their European colleagues of their case, there is a pretty good chance that their proposal will turn into reality. The Norwegians can devise an ideal negotiating position and stick to it without compromising with their European neighbours. But when it comes to the negotiations in Geneva, what chance does little Norway have of prevailing over the United States, Japan, China, India or the European Union?

The basic precondition for democracy is the power to deliver what the people want. If you lose the ability to translate the will of the people and the deliberations of their representatives into changes in the real world, democracy is reduced to a charade.

In Norway there is the appearance of sovereignty because the Norwegian Parliament is technically the highest authority in the country; but the reality is that many of the areas that they discuss are beyond their control. The Parliament is the political equivalent of Robinson Crusoe on his desert island, who, in the words of Geoffrey Howe, was 'sovereign of everything and master of nothing'.[9] Ireland has pooled some of its sovereignty but has regained control of its destiny. European law takes precedence over national law, but that law is made by Irish ministers and Irish members of the European Parliament in collaboration with their European colleagues.

By giving national governments a voice in the world, the European Union has saved national democracy from becoming a mere talking shop that comments on global events while the real decisions are taken elsewhere. The European Union is the only way that small countries can have a measure of control over global markets. This allows nation-states to make their own choices about what to do with their affairs. If you are outside the European Union you must fight tooth and nail to get access to other people's markets, pay huge tariffs for your exports, and try to compete by trimming welfare provisions, employee protection, and tax rates.[10]

The European Union allows you access to a huge market without tariffs and puts you in a strong negotiating position with the rest of the world. But it leaves the really important decisions to national politicians. They set their tax rates. They decide how to spend the money they raise on health, education, and defence. They decide how to redistribute money from rich to poor. The EU creates wealth and the ability to shape events, empowering national politicians – and their citizens – to decide what kind of country they want to live in.

How Europe Empowers Citizens

Europe's greatest gift is choice. The freedom to choose what country to live in, what food to eat, what university to study in, what job to work in, and where to sell your products.

The shelves of every supermarket in Britain groan under the weight of fresh pasta from Italy, French cheeses, Greek olives and Danish bacon. It is not just that fettuccini in mushroom sauce has replaced sausages and beans as a convenience food; all European consumers can now eat the best of European cuisine without having to pay prohibitive prices. The freedom to travel for work or leisure has opened up horizons for millions of people. A pregnant teenager in Dublin can travel to London to have the abortion that is illegal at home. A budding businessman from Prague can go to get an MBA at INSEAD in Paris. A gay couple from Budapest can travel to Copenhagen and get married. A pensioner from Essex can live out her sunset years near a beach in the Costa Blanca.

Because Europeans can take advantage of the best that Europe has to offer, they are asking tougher questions of their own national governments. Commentators have been so focused on the exact distribution of powers between the different institutions in Brussels that they have missed the revolutionary effect that European integration has had on our national political debates.[11]

It wasn't until September 2000 that it became clear how much European citizens were comparing the policies of the different governments in Europe. When French lorry drivers started a blockade over the cost of fuel, the Jospin government was forced to grant them a 15 per cent cut in fuel duty. Within days, copycat protests had spread across Europe. In the Netherlands, truck drivers disrupted traffic around Amsterdam and Rotterdam. In Germany over two hundred lorries, buses, and taxis drove to the border with

France. Belgian drivers continued a third day of action with truckers and taxis setting up barricades in major streets around the city centre and in the southern cities of Charleroi and Nivelles. Irish and Spanish drivers soon added their weight to the wave of protest. In Britain, farmers managed to block off petrol from nearly three-quarters of the UK's 13,000 petrol stations.

Because of the European Union, national governments were being held to account in an entirely new way: their performance is compared with that of their neighbours. Day after day, even Eurosceptic newspapers like the *Daily Mail* were showing that British tax-payers were paying above the European average. Increasingly, this 'European average' pits EU governments against each other in terms of their ability to deliver key services, and gives a touchstone against which citizens can judge their national government's competence.

When a survey showed that fewer Germans reached the top scores for literacy than in twelve of the fifteen European Union states, the government was forced to respond immediately with an investment programme totalling 4 billion to support all-day schooling. Tony Blair has made a commitment to raise health spending to the EU average before 2005, while the Liberal Democrats at their conference in Bournemouth committed to raising spending on all public services to the European average. President Chirac has pledged to reduce the rate of corporation tax to '*la moyenne Européenne*' within five years.

In March 2000, the leaders of the European Union met in Lisbon and agreed to use these comparative statistics to increase the pressure on national governments to perform. They set out a goal of making Europe 'the most competitive and dynamic knowledge-based economy in the world by 2010, capable of sustainable economic growth, with more and better jobs and greater social cohesion'. This was turned into measurable targets for the EU in employment, innovation, economic reform and social cohesion. The performance of each government was monitored by the European Commission so that countries that are performing badly can be named and shamed, and those that do well can be imitated.

So far, progress has been limited, but the fact that people see their national policies within a broader context is already creating a genuine competition for policies across Europe. The European average can be tremendously empowering for citizens. Increasingly, European integration will turn into a progressive quest for the best policies: the finest hospitals, the most creative schools, the most efficient measures against crime.

Escaping the Trap of the Democratic Deficit

The European Union is a laboratory for reinventing democracy.[12] There is still some way to go in creating a 'public space' to debate and resolve pressing problems, where political majorities can emerge, and solutions at the European level can motivate EU citizens. But though Europe's current system of government could be better, it is still the most exciting experiment in democracy in the world.

The problem is that Europe's democratic revolution has

gone largely unnoticed by its citizens. In every member-state, support for the European Union is falling, and on the rare occasions when citizens are asked if they support integration many have answered no, *nej*, or *non*. The near-miss of the French referendum on Maastricht in 1991, the Danish '*Nejs*' in 1991 and 2000, the Irish 'No' in 2002, and the Swedish shake of the head in 2003 have cast a long shadow on the European project.

Stung by the EU's falling popularity, the European leaders launched a 'Constitutional Convention' to explore how Europe could be put back in touch with its citizens. Launched under the chairmanship of the former French President Valéry Giscard d'Estaing, the Convention self-consciously modelled itself on the Philadelphia Convention at which James Madison, Benjamin Franklin, and George Washington hammered out the modern American Constitution, endowing it with a directly elected president, a senate and a house of representatives, a supreme court, and a clear division of powers.[13] But the solutions they came up with were very different from the ones dreamt up by their American forefathers.

Many of their proposals will help to make Europe more open and efficient. The Constitution will throw European decision-making open to the public by insisting that the European Council meets in public session when it is passing legislation. It allows the EU to deliver more effectively in the global arena by creating a European Foreign Minister. It sets limits on European integration by allowing a third of national parliaments to block any Commission proposal. And most intriguingly, it introduces an element of direct democracy: for the first time there is a right to petition the

Commission to make proposals by collecting a million signatures.

But what is even more interesting are the measures they didn't propose. After 16 months of deliberations, 26 meetings of the Convention plenary over 52 days, dozens of meetings of working groups, 1,800 speeches, 1,500 written contributions, 6,000 amendments and 21 million euros-worth of expenses,[14] they produced a draft Constitution that explicitly rejected the American model. Many people had argued that Europe should develop a presidential or parliamentary system modelled on the nation-state. But these critics were missing the point of the European Union.

The reason that people do not turn out in their droves to vote for the European Parliament is not because it has no power. It is because none of the issues in which the EU specializes – trade liberalization, monetary policy, the removal of non-tariff barriers, technical regulation in the environmental and other areas, foreign aid, and general foreign policy co-ordination – appears anywhere on the list of issues that voters care about.[15] In fact, none of the policies in the five most important issues for voters in Europe – health care provision, education, law and order, pension and social security policy, and taxation – are set by the European Union. So, with a focus on technical issues and very little power over the services that Europeans care about, a directly elected President of Europe would have no more chance of inspiring European citizens than one appointed by European governments and the European Parliament.

And even if people could be persuaded to vote for a president, the outcome would be disastrous. There never will be a central figure or body like a president, prime minister or parliament solely responsible for setting the European agenda and driving it forward because European citizens would not accept their national governments being 'lorded over' by an EU president or parliament. The strength of 'Network Europe' is that, although different countries may have different weights on different issues, none, however powerful, can ignore the others. This is why national governments and peoples have come to accept the EU. Its fragile legitimacy would be shattered if individual countries felt consistently ignored – just as many Scots began to question the viability of a United Kingdom that seemed to have a perpetual Conservative government, in spite of the fact that Scots voted Labour in large numbers.

The Convention recognized that aping the American Constitution by creating a directly elected President of the Commission or a European Parliament with the power to elect a European executive or initiate legislation would destroy the things that make Europe work: its flexibility to evolve in order to tackle new problems; its multiple centres of power so that all member-states have their interests represented; its respect for national democracy and identity.

The European Constitution is not poetry. It has none of the drama of the American Constitution because it is not a text designed to establish a nation-state. But it does enshrine the principles of 'Network Europe', which is now free to carry on its unique experiment of reinventing democracy for an age of globalization.

CHAPTER 8

Europe at 50

The French writer Alexis de Tocqueville is best known for his tour of America and the missives he sent back about the fledgling democracy in the 1830s. However, in 1837, de Tocqueville set off on another perilous sea journey in search of new types of governance – this time across the Mediterranean rather than the Atlantic. On 22 August he penned a letter to his friend from Algeria about the perils of imperialism: 'Suppose ... the emperor of China, landing on the shores of France and at the head of a powerful army, made himself master of our greatest cities and of our capital. And after having destroyed all of the public registers before even having given himself the pain of reading them, destroyed or dispersed all administrators without acquainting himself with their various attributes, he finally rids himself of all state officials from the head of the government to the *gardes champêtres*.'[1] De Tocqueville argues that the powerful army, fortresses and fortune would be of no help in governing a land with a different religion, language, and laws. The result would be a mix of militarized occupation in some parts of the country and anarchy in the rest: 'You will see, Sir, that we have done in Algeria precisely what I supposed the emperor of China would do in France.'

A hundred and seventy years later, Algeria continues to live in the purgatory he describes: neither able to throw off the authoritarian model of government it inherited from its colonial past, nor allowed to attempt self-government for fear that Islamists might come to power. The cancer of authoritarianism continues to blight the country with the tacit support of its former colonial power. And what is true in Algeria is true for many of Europe's new neighbours to the south and east. In North Africa and the Middle East, semi-authoritarian regimes continue to rule with the support of the West, while in former Soviet states, like Belarus and Moldova, autocratic rulers keep a handle on simmering ethnic disputes with support from their former Russian rulers.

The European project now faces its moment of truth: how to have the same transformative effect on its new neighbours as it had on Central and Eastern Europe and Turkey. How to turn a European Union of twenty-five members into a community of fifty democracies that transforms its neighbours in its wake.

The British and Americans – for different reasons and in a different age – are reliving de Tocqueville's nightmare in Iraq. They are trying to turn the country into a viable democratic state but, having swept everything away, are having to rebuild everything from scratch, from electricity and water through police and postal codes to ministries and municipal dustbins. This is the hard way to build democracy: working against the grain, replacing local systems with ones imported from outside, having to occupy and control everything to make sure it does not descend into chaos. In a single year, the United States is spending more on reconstructing a country with 20 million people than the European Union spent on bringing democracy to the entire former Soviet bloc in a decade.[2]

The difference is clear: the European idea of democracy has not travelled in armoured convoys from the west. It is an ideal that inspires people to change themselves from the inside. But can Europe pull it off again?

Hunger for Change

In the flower market in downtown Tbilisi, sales of roses are booming. Roses became the symbol of a revolution that swept through Georgia in November 2003. The demonstrators against a flawed election did not injure a single person – they were armed with red roses rather than guns or Molotov cocktails. As they gathered outside the Parliament, the President, Eduard Shevardnadze, deployed hundreds of soldiers onto the streets. But when the protesting students handed their roses to the soldiers, many laid down their guns. The leader of the revolution, Mikhail Saakashvili, a US-educated 35-year-old, handed the sitting president a rose, and shouted 'Resign!' Within months, he was elected by a landslide: securing more than 96 per cent of the vote.[3] His promise to the people of Georgia was to bring the country into the European mainstream: 'The new members of the EU have made it very clear that they are not closing the doors

101

behind them. We have made progress and we are working on it every day. We are going for it, whatever it takes. The EU should welcome us and wait for us.'[4] While the Georgians demonstrated, others watched. A year later their neighbours in Ukraine launched an 'Orange Revolution' in similar circumstances, with the reformist leader Viktor Yushchenko basing his campaign on the promise of a European future. But the echoes of the events in Tbilisi were felt much further afield.

Throughout the Arab world, the media buzzed with envy. In Lebanon, *Al-Nahar* columnist Sahar Ba'asiri called on her compatriots to take note of events in Tbilisi: 'Watching the "flower revolution" in Georgia on television, I felt envious ... The crowds massing at [the parliament building] to carry out their will pained me – as if they and we Arabs lived on different planets, and on our planet none know the meaning of the will of the peoples.'[5] In a column criticizing the Arab elite, Sa'ad Mahyew wrote in the UAE daily *Al-Khaleej*: 'Why aren't Arab societies experiencing revolutions similar [to Georgia's]? Why are they comatose while all the peoples of the world – including those of Africa – have since 1989 been dancing to the rhythm of a single genuine and universal revolution sweeping [the world] towards the mill of democracy? Why has the Arab region still not sprouted democratic and liberal movements offering the Arab peoples an alternative to the existing variety of despotism and authoritarian regimes?'[6]

The big problem is how to translate people's desire for change into real reform. There are limits to what can be done from the outside. When the United States launched its 'Middle East Partnership Initiative' which sought to reward reform with aid and trade opportunities, the response was damning. In an article titled 'Yes to Democracy, No to the US, Hussein Abd Al-Razaq, columnist for the Egyptian opposition daily *Al-Ahali*, wrote: 'The American administration's talk of democracy is deception that can fool no one. It is the US that toppled Allende's democratic regime in Chile and set up Pinochet's dictatorship in its stead. Today, it is the one attempting to bring down the democratically elected Chavez government in Venezuela. Its alliance with the despotic regimes in the Arab world is well known.'[7] Suspicions are so great that even when the United States adopts policies that should command support in the region, they run into a wall of suspicion. A story, published in the Egyptian paper *Al-Ahram*, claimed that American humanitarian aid to Afghanistan had been genetically modified and deliberately dropped in heavily land-mined areas, presumably with the aim of killing or injuring Afghan civilians.

Europeans certainly have a better image in the region than the USA. They have learned the hard way not to couch their aims in terms of a 'civilizing mission', and Jacques Chirac's opposition to the Iraq war saw him come second only to Osama Bin Laden in a poll of popular leaders in the Arab world. But the identity of the messenger is only part of the problem. The main advantage of a European approach is that it should be a response to local demands. The European Union can do this because it is not just another country telling the Arabs and Eastern Europeans how to run their affairs: it is a club with rules and benefits to hand out. By couching their relations in terms of creating a neighbourhood club – and exploring what rules the club should adhere to –

they can create the incentives to drive reform without being imperial.

Keeping the Door Open

As the moment of truth approaches, many are baulking at Europe's destiny. Just as they talk of Turkey as a 'model' for the Middle East, they are explicitly ruling out the very thing that inspired Turkey to change: the possibility of joining the European club.

Today, the list of prospective members is long. Romania, Bulgaria and Turkey are already engaged in accession negotiations. The Western Balkans are preparing for membership. The Ukrainian and Georgian governments have declared their intention of pursuing it; Morocco has twice expressed an interest in joining; Silvio Berlusconi held out the prospect of full membership to Russia on a recent visit and there were a number of discussions within Israeli political circles in 2001–2 about whether the EU could provide an 'anchor' for Israel in any move towards a negotiated two-state settlement with Palestine.

But Europe's response has been uncertain. The former Commission President, Romano Prodi, said that Ukraine 'has as much reason to be in the EU as New Zealand'. When Morocco expressed an interest in joining the European Union in 1987, it was rapidly rebuffed on the grounds that it is not European. Smarting from the rejection, King Hassan of Morocco openly complained in 1994 that '[Europeans] look for allies more to the East, because there people are white ... because it's one big family. And then they look across the

Mediterranean and say "Ah yes, it's true, there are those poor little people that we colonized".[8] Europe's focus is naturally on digesting the last wave of enlargement, and preparing for Turkey, rather than looking forward to another 'Big Bang'.

But as we found with the Balkans in the early 1990s, Europe's security cannot be guaranteed by re-erecting an iron curtain.[9] The choice is to get involved with our neighbours now and create the incentives for them to change – or to face the potentially violent consequences of collapse later and pay a much higher price then. Each wave of enlargement poses a new challenge, as no country wants to be surrounded by chaos. In the same way that the Germans wanted Poland in the club so that their neighbour would be stable, the Poles now want the Ukrainians to join. When they themselves join, they will want to bring Belarus with them.

There is a debate about the ethics and effectiveness of raising false expectations of membership: French and German promises that Poland would join the EU by 2000 contributed to later Polish perceptions that the EU had dragged its feet. The Turks are suspicious of the EU's intentions because they can see that European leaders say one thing to Turkish audiences and another to their own domestic constituencies.[10]

But there is a greater danger than raising expectations: categorically ruling out membership. As long as there is hope for entry, and a clear path to achieve it, there are incentives for change. At various times people have tried to define Europe's borders, but the membership of the European Union is ultimately self-selecting. In 1989 people vacillated about whether Europe should concentrate on deepening or widening – whether it could absorb the poor countries of

Central and Eastern Europe; but once the countries agreed to obey the rules of the club, it was morally untenable to exclude them.

The point is not to offer membership – that is clearly unrealistic for many of Europe's new neighbours – but we should certainly not close off the possibility. We must be fuzzy about where the borders of the Union will lie, but crystal clear about what countries need to do to hope to join. We must make it clear to them that whether they want to join the European Union or create a Mediterranean free trade area, there will be huge incentives from the European Union for countries that strengthen the rule of law, respect human rights, and adopt the *acquis communautaire*. This is the only way to reverse the toxic dynamic of relations with our neighbours. Instead of us being seen to be imposing our political norms from the outside, they need to be asking us for engagement.[11]

The Ring of Friends

The former President of the European Commission, Romano Prodi, has spoken of turning this potential zone of instability on the EU's fringes into a 'ring of friends'.[12] He said that these countries would be offered everything short of membership. The strategy which the European Commission published lists fifteen incentives ranging from 'more effective political dialogue' to 'perspectives of integration into transport, energy and communications networks' and 'enlarged and improved [financial] assistance'.

Already the Commission has negotiated detailed 'Action

Plans' with five countries, listing 200 concrete political and economic reforms that they need to meet in exchange for rewards from the European Union.[13] Importantly, these are not just agreements with the governments – it would be wrong to have high hopes of the democratic enthusiasm of leaders like Hosni Mubarak in Egypt, Zine el Abidine Ben Ali in Tunisia, or Bashir Assad in Syria. One of the conditions of the agreements is that they are drawn up in consultation with local civil societies. Countries that sign up to these agreements become eligible for a 'political premium' (5 per cent of MEDA funds have informally been set aside for this purpose).[14]

This is an exciting new initiative which could drive a process of reform in Europe's near-abroad. However, for all the talk of partnership, the relationship that is being offered is one of dependence. There is a danger that the package will be seen as a placebo for membership rather than a pathway to eventually joining the club. In the medium term, if the EU really wants to transform its neighbourhood, it should consider creating a new political community that these countries will have a say in governing: a Euro-Mediterranean Free Trade area – with an understanding that they might eventually join the club.

Europe at Fifty

Many will argue that the European Union would be unworkable at fifty, that going beyond the current twenty-five members will be a recipe for gridlock and over-stretch. But the EU is a dynamic political system that is already grappling with the challenge of diversity and continental reach. If Europe continues to grow, it is clear that it will become a series of overlapping communities that share the 80,000 pages of the *acquis communautaire* but do not work together on everything else. There are already three ambitious projects that do not include all of the EU's 25 members: the eurozone, which only twelve countries have joined; the Schengen agreement, which allows passport free travel between 15 countries; and the Western European Union, Europe's defence identity, which has 10 full members.

If ever there was a cause to listen to Monnet's injunction to 'enlarge the context by changing the basic facts' it is in Europe's new neighbourhood. If Europe was the incubator of war and instability in the twentieth century, Europe's new neighbours are the home of some of the greatest threats to international security in the twenty-first century.[15]

This will be the biggest test of European foreign policy. All the more so because Europe is not the only pole of attraction in this region. To the east there is an increasingly assertive Russian Republic, which is emboldened by economic growth and using its vast natural resources to reclaim a global role for itself and build an empire of energy-dependent neighbours. To the south and the east there is a considerable American presence. There are US military bases in Iraq, Kuwait, Bahrain, Oman, Israel, Qatar, the United Arab Emirates, Uzbekistan, Tajikistan and Kyrgyzstan, as well as plans for a new 'family of bases' in Romania, Poland, Bulgaria, Morocco, Tunisia, and Algeria[16]. The USA will always have an important say in decisions in the region, not least because it is also an important economic partner to many countries and is signing free trade agreements with them.

This makes it all the more important for Europeans to show that they can take responsibility for their near-abroad, and work with the Americans to develop a new approach, as they did in Central and Eastern Europe. In all the major countries, we can point to a different way forward.

For example, in Iran, American strategies of isolation and coercion are actually encouraging the suppression of democracy and the development of nuclear weapons. The lesson the Iranians drew from the Iraq war is that the only way to be safe from American invasion is to have a nuclear deterrent – and the challenge is to develop it quickly while American troops are still bogged down in Iraq. Equally, as Iran has already become a 'pariah state', it has nothing to lose by suppressing democracy. This is why a European policy, which starts with a recognition of Iran's motivations and tries to change the calculus of risk for the government, could be more effective. By taking their security concerns seriously, and offering major economic benefits, it is trying to regain leverage over the Iranian regime that the American strategy of isolation has lost. But without American involvement the EU cannot succeed as it cannot offer the Iranians the security guarantees they need.

In the Arab world and the Caucasus, Bush's war on terror has actually consolidated autocratic regimes – from Mubarak in Egypt to Nazarbayev in Kazakhstan – which are using the cloak of counter-terrorism to justify a strengthening of their grip over the media and a systematic policy of arresting and discriminating against their political opponents. Equally, the American policy of creating bilateral free trade areas has already complicated European schedules to create a regional free trade zone and to harness the emerging regionalism as a key part of its democracy promotion policy.

In all these places Europe can deploy its 'transformative power' to shape the parts of societies that America cannot reach with the magnet of its neighbourhood policy, and the link between market access and political reform. The decision to start negotiations with Turkey has now removed a taboo about religion and geography and shown that the European Union is, above all, a community of values.

As the former French finance minister, Dominique Strauss-Kahn, says: 'after opening to the East, Europe must now turn to the South so that it can again become the link between the Western World and the Orient ... We will have to think about how to make it possible for countries from the ex-Soviet Union and the Mediterranean Basin, such as those of the Maghreb, to join our political area.' It might be too early, as he says, to start preparing for a European Union that stretches from the icebergs of the Arctic North to the sand dunes of the Sahara, with the Mediterranean in their midst. But it would be criminal to rule it out.

CHAPTER 9

Brussels and the Beijing Consensus

In my local curry house I was greeted like a long-lost friend. A huddle of young waiters gesticulated excitedly towards me. Eventually I realized they were pointing at my bag, picked up during a recent trip to China, and emblazoned with the Chinese script for Shanghai. 'You've been to China,' they said. 'China have just put a man in space ... they're taking over from America.'

These young Bengalis are not just motivated by regional passions. Everywhere in the developing world people are sitting up and taking notice of the Chinese juggernaut. As a model for development it is a source of inspiration, its giddy growth rates of over 8 per cent a year[1] lifting millions of people out of poverty. But even more exciting is the prospect of a new superpower that might challenge US hegemony and the American way of doing things.

People are already talking of the 'Chinese Century' and the 'Beijing Consensus' because China's emergence does not fit the textbook model of Western development. The People's Republic is not driven by a desire to make the bankers of the IMF and the World Bank happy, but by the more fundamental urge for equitable, high-quality growth. It treats the ideas of privatization and free trade with caution rather than pursuing them with zeal. Its foreign policy is driven by a fierce defence of national borders and interests, and an increasing commitment to multilateral institutions such as the United Nations. Together these policies have allowed China to grow without losing its independence to such financial institutions as the World Bank and the IMF, global companies, or the Bush administration.[2]

Faced with China's bewildering size and rate of growth, many will feel that China's emergence will eclipse Europe's transformative power. But China's secret is that as it grows and asserts itself on the world stage, it is becoming ever more like the European Union: Chinese development is driven by a desire to escape from historical trauma. The political establishment puts peace and stability above all else. An interventionist state seeks to marry economic dynamism with social cohesion. In foreign policy the Chinese believe in building global institutions such as the United Nations and the international rule of law. And in Asia, China is driving a process of regional integration in its neighbourhood that could one day create a European Union of the East.

The extraordinary fact that few people have picked up on is that China's rise in the world could be one of the key drivers of the 'New European Century'.

'Emerging Precipitously in a Peaceful Way'

The seaside resort of Boao is situated on the east coast of China's Hainan Island, surrounded by sandy beaches, coconut trees, and hot springs. It was here, on 3 November 2003, that the former Central Party School Vice-President Zheng Bijian chose to go public with his idea of the 'peaceful rise of China'.[3]

Because China's modern history is marked by humiliation inflicted by foreign powers and civil wars, government officials have talked for years of the 'rejuvenation of the Chinese nation'[4] to rally their citizens. But while this phrase plays well with domestic audiences it sends shivers down the spines of China's neighbours, who don't want to become roadkill in the path of a Chinese juggernaut. The 'Peaceful Rise' theory was explicitly designed to counter the idea that China's emergence would be a threat. The concept was the product of an intensive study commissioned by the State Council and carried out by PhD students from Shanghai. They looked at forty case studies of development and discovered that the most successful rises were accompanied by stability and a peaceful international environment.

Peaceful Rise, or *heping jueqi* (literally, 'emerging precipitously in a peaceful way'), sums up Beijing's avowed goal of good neighbourliness and global responsibility. Beijing has stressed that, far from hurting other nations, China's rise will bring them sizeable gains. Chinese theorists like to stress that, while the economic strength of Japan and the other Asian dragons was based on aggressive, even predatory exports, China's growth can be attributed not just to overseas markets but also to massive domestic consumption and foreign investment.[5] As China has opened its door to imports, which increased by more than 40 per cent last year, Chinese growth has acted as an economic booster not just to its region, but to the whole world.

Certainly, the Chinese have gone to great lengths to communicate their desire for peace. In recent years, they have resolved virtually all land border disputes with their neighbours. They signed a non-aggression pact with ASEAN, which means that sovereignty disputes over flashpoints such as the South China Sea would be shelved indefinitely in the interest of joint economic development. They are working earnestly to help resolve the North Korean nuclear issue. Through means that include free trade agreements, the Chinese leadership also pledged to boost imports from, and economic aid to, ASEAN countries.[6] They have conducted joint military exercises with Russia, Kyrgyzstan, India, and Pakistan to build trust with their neighbours.[7]

China is also trying hard to avoid a confrontation with the United States. Since the spat early in Bush's first term when a US spy plane and a Chinese fighter collided, relations have thawed. After 11 September, Beijing provided Washington with useful intelligence and, like Russia, used it as an excuse to damn their own separatist movements. The Chinese have played an active role in North Korea through the 'six party talks', which bring together the United Nations, Japan, South Korea and the Democratic People's Republic of Korea. Even over Iraq, the Chinese supported the first UN resolution and kept a low profile, unlike during Kosovo, when Chinese spokesmen were on a 24-hour rota condemning NATO's illegal action. The Chinese have also used their $400 billion of foreign reserves to buy up dollars and government bonds, creating a deep economic interdependence between China and the USA.

Although there has been a backlash against the phrase 'Peaceful Rise' in the People's Republic, with the President Hu Jintao and the Prime Minister Wen Jiabao quietly replacing it with 'Peaceful Development',[8] this has more to do with the internal politics of the Communist Party than China's strategic outlook. The ideas behind the notion, of regional integration, multilateralism, and avoiding conflict, are already setting a new direction for Chinese foreign policy. What is more, the strategy seems to be working. Robert W. Radtke, writing in the *Christian Science Monitor,* shows how China's soft sell is managing to appeal to US allies in the region: 'China's Peaceful Rise was introduced to Asia by Chinese President Hu Jintao on his tour of Southeast Asia in October – just on the heels of President Bush's visit to the region that month. The contrast in tone between the two leaders couldn't have been more striking. In short, China's message was, "We're here to help," while the US message was "You're either with us or against us" in the war on terror. It's not hard to imagine which was the more effective diplomatic strategy.'[9]

Network China

The second big change has been Chinese support for multilateralism. Only a few years ago, the Chinese regarded all multilateral institutions as instruments of Western imperialism. This is not surprising given China's early experience of them: Beijing was not only refused a seat at the United Nations until 1971, it was also a target of UN sanctions during the Korean War in the 1950s.[10]

The spur for the change of heart has been twofold. Initially, the motivations were economic: China gradually realized that it had become the greatest beneficiary of globalization after the USA. This led Deng Xiao Ping to advocate a policy of 'recognizing the existing international system to ensure a benign environment conducive to domestic economic development'.[11] The second spur was the inexorable rise of America after the end of the Cold War.

Seen from Beijing, the greatest danger today is not of the international organizations interfering in China but the USA's undermining of international organizations in the security field. The Chinese Foreign Minister Li Zhaoxing recently argued: 'Countries, big or small, strong or weak, are equal before international law and basic norms governing international relations. The existing international multilateral institutions, with the United Nations at its core, is the best venue for all countries to participate in international affairs on an equal footing and the institutional guarantee for democratic and law-based international relations. We have every reason to strengthen it and no excuse to weaken it.'[12]

That is why China, like the EU, is slowly grappling with how global institutions can be reformed for new challenges. On a recent trip to China, I was told that the People's Republic might even reconsider its opposition to the principle of intervention in other countries' internal affairs and accept limited cases of 'humanitarian intervention'.

The most remarkable shift in Chinese policy has been China's espousal of regional integration. Chinese scholars have studied the European model to see how they can recast their relationship with their neighbours. Four years after the end of the Soviet Union, China and its neighbours to the west – Russia, Kazakhstan, Kyrgyzstan and Tajikistan – came together to negotiate their new borders in a coalition called the 'Shanghai Five'. They negotiated treaties demilitarizing the 4,300-mile border that they share and gradually expanded their co-operation to include security and trade. In 2001, when Uzbekistan joined, the 'Shanghai Five' became the 'Shanghai Co-operation Organization'. This new organization has already created a 'Regional Anti-terrorism Structure' in Uzbekistan, and organized co-operation on economic, border, and law enforcement matters – as well as two combined military exercises. Regional analysts talk of a 'Shanghai spirit' emerging – principles of mutual trust, mutual benefit and equality – and bringing stability to the region.[13]

To the south and east, a similar revolution has taken hold. Throughout the Cold War period China's interactions with ASEAN states were conducted solely on a bilateral basis. However, over the last fifteen years, its passion for regional integration has come to resemble the European Union's. Chinese leaders are talking of forming an 'Asian community', like the European Union and including an Asian currency, based on the Chinese yuan, so as not to rely on the dollar.[14]

Of course China's fractious relationship with Japan will continue to hold things up. Memories of the Second World War run deep, and both sides have stoked up popular antipathy. The Japanese Prime Minister's annual visit to honour Japanese soldiers convicted of war crimes in China ensures an annual upsurge of hostility, while the Chinese state-controlled media lose few opportunities to encourage anti-Japanese sentiment. However, some experts believe that the ongoing momentum of regional economic co-operation, the recovery of Japan's economy, and the two countries' shared interest in resolving the North Korea nuclear issue could bring them together.[15]

Europe's Chinese Challenge

The 'European China' I describe is only one of a number of possible worlds. Its emergence will depend on two major shifts in Chinese thinking. First, the development of a new ethic of global responsibility. In the last year China has played a key role in North Korea, it has shown itself more willing to take part in discussions about global governance, and has committed a limited number of troops to UN peace-keeping missions. But to be a partner to Europe in the political sphere as well as the economic one, China will have to get involved in a meaningful way in stabilizing failed states, protecting people from genocide, tackling global warming, and preventing the proliferation of WMD. China will also need to shift its thinking on sovereignty. Rather than seeing pooling sovereignty as a threat, it will need to embrace it further if its attempts at fostering regional integration are to take off.

There are many things that could stand in the way. The resurgent nationalism of public opinion and the 'One China' policy that aims to stop Taiwan from declaring its independence at 'any price' are frightening to European observers. The Chinese government's voracious appetite for energy is also in danger of pitting China against some of the European Union's priorities. Its need to protect its energy interests in Sudan and Iran could put Beijing at odds with Western attempts to halt genocide in the former and the proliferation of WMD in the latter. The biggest question mark continues to be over democracy and human rights. There has been a growing move to create a more meritocratic system within the Communist Party and attempts to open it up to successful people from business. There is talk of the next big revolution being one of democracy, with elections being introduced at city and state level. However, this will be a long-term process.

The way that China turns out will depend in part on how it is treated. If it is treated as a threat, as many neo-conservative thinkers are wont to do, it is possible that the prophecy will be self-fulfilling. An attempt to contain China and thwart its development could drive its nationalism and provoke a disastrous war over Taiwan. Equally, if the developed world treats China as a partner and binds it into global institutions, it is possible that the People's Republic will become wrapped up in its own multilateralist logic. China's embrace of the market has led to its commitment to a peaceful ideology and multilateralism. It is likely that these policies in turn will unleash their own dynamic and consequently redefine China's ideas of its national interests, security, and even identity, in the same way that Britain, France, and Germany have been changed by the lived experience of multilateralism.

As it emerges as a global superpower, China's multi-lateralism will not only reshape the dynamic of its own region. It could also have a dramatic impact on other great powers. Bill Clinton is convinced that the growing power of China will force his own country to reconsider its commitment to multilateralism: 'The United States stands at a unique moment in human history, with our political, economic and military dominance. But within 30 years the Chinese economy could be as big or bigger than ours ... Then, in an interdependent world, we can lead but not dominate.'[16] He hopes that when America is faced with China's rise, it will be driven to embrace a world ruled by international law rather than military force.

If all goes well, China could be one of the most important agents of transformative power, adapting Europe's recipe for success to its own region and helping build a global environment that embodies multilateralism and regional integration. Ironically, the lasting legacy of China's rise might be a 'New European Century'.

CHAPTER 10

The End of the American World Order

Washington prepares for an airborne invasion every seventeen years. The cicadas descend on the nation's capital and the eastern states like a biblical plague. They hatch, crawl out of the ground, mate, lay eggs, and then disappear for another seventeen years. Observing them, a European living in the imperial capital in 2004, I've come to see their lurch from orgies of activism to retrenchment as a metaphor for American foreign policy. The French writer Raymond Aron once described American policy as a series of 'swings between the crusading spirit and a withdrawal into isolation far from a corrupt world that refused to heed the American Gospel'.[1]

Since 1945, we have become accustomed to the warm glow of the crusading spirit. During the Cold War, the United States embraced 'entangling alliances' in Europe and Asia; deployed troops around the world to maintain the balance of power; and helped build global economic and political institutions that upheld the values of liberal democracy. The United Nations, the IMF, the World Bank, NATO, and even the European Union, were nurtured and funded by American presidents. Now this orgy of engagement is coming to an end.

Although President Bush actually called his war on terror a 'crusade', his period in office has seen the United States pioneer a new kind of isolationism, designed for the age of Bill Gates and Osama Bin Laden. America has not retreated from the world – its economy and security are too dependent on global events – but it has tried to break free from the world order that it created. Between 11 September 2001 and June 2004, US military spending grew to match that of the whole of the rest of the world combined. Meanwhile, Washington initiated a bonfire of international agreements, jeopardizing Kyoto, the International Criminal Court, the ABM and Biological Weapons treaties. The USA also highlighted its capacity for wars and military occupations. This trinity of American military supremacy, unilateralism, and pre-emptive war has been heralded as the 'Bush Revolution' that will define an assertive foreign policy for a generation.

Much has been written on the nature of transatlantic divisions, and what steps might be taken to heal them in the short term, but the purpose of this book is to look beyond the next few years at the shape of the world order over the course of the century. The 'Bush Revolution' is based on the false premise that being the only superpower means that you can do what you like. It has damaged America's standing in the world, squandered its power, and brought with it a period of self-enforced isolation. But, as Aron suggests, this strategic outlook will not last. America's ambition, and its need for security, will lead it to return to the world long before the generation is finished.

So what will this world look like?

The end of the Cold War and the rise of globalization have unleashed three major shifts in global power: from countries in the West to those in the East; from an order organized around the rights of states to one that embraces the protection of individuals from global threats like genocide, terrorism, and global warming; and from a system whose pinnacle was national power to one increasingly defined by regional integration.

With this transformation under way, the transatlantic relationship can never be revived in its old form. But if Europe lays out a template for a new world order, it can work with the Americans to create an alliance that goes beyond the two continents, enlisting new allies in a quest to solve global problems. This is a far more compelling vision than defining Europe against America. As Timothy Garton Ash and others have argued, instead of trying to contain America to prevent the next Iraq, we must recognise that our goal should be working with an engaged internationalist America to re-invent the world order for a new era.[2]

If Europe succeeds, it could transform the nature of American power for a post-American world.

The Rise of the South and the East

It is no longer possible for 90 per cent of the world's population to be governed by a system designed to suit the interests of Europe and America. As the century moves on, the centre of gravity will move inexorably from the North and West to the East and South. The fruits of economic globalization could allow China and India to overtake the USA in economic terms by the middle of the century, with Brazil, Russia, and South Africa following fast behind.

Their ascendancy is already sending shockwaves through the global economic system. China, with its $440 billion of foreign reserves,[3] has bought up $5 billion of US government bonds, while India has amassed over $100 billion of reserves;[4] their need for natural resources is driving up global prices; and their development is triggering a series of new environmental problems. As their economies develop, the new tigers of the South and East will also develop greater political, military, and cultural power.

The decline of American 'soft power' is possibly the most dramatic sign of the end of the American century. The tension between 'Brand America' and Pax Americana has driven advertising agencies like McCann Erickson to advise their clients not to wrap their products in the American flag.[5] Of course the American dream still has a powerful draw, but it is being challenged by the rise of Bollywood, Al-Jazeera, European brands, and the Chinese model of development. The fact that Japanese and Korean kids learnt to play baseball in the 1950s was part of a national desire to see these two countries as part of the American world. But without a Soviet threat to hold that world together, the identity of the West is starting to fragment.

As countries like India, Brazil, and South Africa rise it will be impossible to shut them out of the cockpit of global power. All the institutions of the American Era – from the United Nations Security Council and the IMF to the G7 and

NATO – will need to be opened up if they are not to sink into irrelevance and lose legitimacy in an increasingly multipolar world. Neither Europe nor America will be able to resist this in the long term, because to do so would be to attract the hostility of some of the most powerful potential political allies, and the biggest economic markets in the world.

That is why the solipsistic obsession – on both sides of the Atlantic – with the relationship between Europe and America is unhelpful. The challenge now is to bind these emerging powers into a system that reflects the values of democracy, human rights, and open markets. A radical solution would be to create a new dividing line in global politics: democracy. Ivo Daalder and James Lindsay, two former members of the Clinton administration, advocate the creation of an 'Alliance of Democratic States', which would work on everything from combating terrorism to halting global warming.[6] In exchange for meeting democratic standards, its members would get access to a market without tariffs and other barriers; 'just as the prospect of joining NATO and the European Union remade the face of Europe, so too could the prospect of joining the Alliance of Democratic States help remake the world'.[7] The idea of a new alliance of states based on American leadership that does not take regional groupings into account would not be acceptable to the rest of the world. But the concept of linking global power to domestic political behaviour is an obvious extension of the European success story, which could have dramatic implications for the reform of the United Nations, G8, and the WTO.

However, we must recognize that simply adding extra seats to the table of global institutions, for example including Brazil, India or South Africa on the UN Security Council, will not be enough to stop global institutions from falling into irrelevance. These institutions are equipped for a world organized around states, at a time when many global threats come from groups of terrorists, armed militia, or the behaviour of companies.

The Rise of the Individual

The gut-wrenching sight of genocide erupting in Rwanda, Kosovo, and the Sudan tells us that there is something wrong with an international system that places the right of states to be free from military intervention over the rights of the individuals that live in them. And with September 11, we came to see the individual not just as a victim, but as a threat. If a group of nineteen people can inflict so much pain, suffering, and disorder on the world for less than the cost of a single tank, we need to ask serious questions of our definitions of security.

The big success of the end of the twentieth century was to make war between states less likely. The institutions of the American order were designed to prevent the biggest threat to our security: stopping other countries from using their armies to interfere in our internal affairs. But in the twenty-first century, many of the most important threats are neither caused by nor aimed at states: they are about mobile individuals in an era of globalization. Today, we fear invading armies less than terrorism, global warming, the spread of diseases like Aids, or mass migrations caused by ethnic cleansing. With the spread of democracy and human rights around the world, cheap travel, and the telescopic vision of a global media and campaigning organizations that bring suffering into our living rooms, the public is no longer insulated from disasters in distant parts of the globe.

To deal with these new threats of globalization, states need to intervene in each other's internal affairs: to agree global standards to control the emission of greenhouse gases; to share intelligence on terrorists and extradite suspects to other countries; to stop armed militias from committing genocide; and to punish war criminals for their acts of violence. But many countries continue to cling to an international system designed to stop a war between states, and a United Nations Charter that made it illegal to intervene in Kosovo.

The United States recognizes that the system it created is broken, but its solutions are taking us in precisely the wrong direction. In many ways, the Bush Revolution is more of a counter-revolution – an attempt to turn the clock back to a world of states. As John O'Sullivan has argued, Bill Clinton had been developing a foreign policy outlook based around the idea of managing globalization, the importance of non-state actors, humanitarian intervention in Bosnia and Kosovo, and promoting the rule of international law and the International Criminal Court, which had initially been an American idea.

In a matter of months, George W. Bush did all he could to reverse that trend. In hundreds of speeches in office, Bush has never once used the word globalization. According to Richard Clarke, Bush's former counter-terrorism adviser, he refused to focus on terrorism before September 11. Even after the attacks, the cover letter President Bush submitted along with the National Security Strategy identifies its main objectives as 'fighting terrorists and tyrants'. The implication is that if you can remove tyrants such as Saddam Hussein or the Taliban, you can destroy terrorism, because no state will want to take the risk of harbouring them. By associating terrorists with tyrants, it is clear the emphasis is not on individuals – whose actions may not be linked to nation or statehood – but on the old threat of rogue states. The war on terrorism has focused more on deterring the states that house terrorists than it has on dealing with removing the causes that lead individuals to embrace terror in the first place.

The Bush Administration's biggest fear is that international treaties and institutions will curtail America's freedom of action. Its obduracy on terrorism is replicated in its opposition to treaties on global warming, war crimes, and nuclear proliferation. There is some justification to some of their concerns. For example, it is true that it is easy for countries that never send troops abroad to support an International Criminal Court while American troops will face politically motivated trials. But rather than suggesting improvements to the measures developed by the rest of the world, this administration has chosen to remain aloof from them, and to do its best to scupper their development.

America's current stance will ultimately be self-defeating. Denying the existence of non-state threats by translating them into state-based ones will not stop terrorism, global warming, or Aids from threatening American security. And relying mainly on national military power to solve global political problems will not work in the long term. But the biggest reason why America will have to embrace this new world order is that the world will build it anyway. By removing itself from the negotiations, it will lose the ability to shape the outcomes around American interests.

Even in the face of American opposition, Europe can take a lead in creating an order that prioritizes individuals over states. In the 1980s, Communism in Eastern Europe was partly eroded by dissidents who exploited the human rights clauses in the Helsinki Final Act to demand rights from their states. Today, the European Court of Human Rights and European Court of Justice are potential models for the next generation of international justice institutions. Building on the experience of Kosovo, we should campaign for the United Nations Charter to be rewritten to recognize the international community's 'responsibility to protect' citizens from genocide. The European Union is also using its economic power to accelerate the creation of new institutions, by making aid and market access conditional on signing the Kyoto Protocol or recognizing the International Criminal Court.

We should not overestimate either our capacity to achieve such transformations or our legitimacy in doing so. That is why we will need to enlist the support of regional organizations behind these goals.

The Rise of the Regions

The American world order is based around nation-states at a time when regions are coming together. The United States does not have the resources or the will to be a global policeman, and many parts of the world would rather deal with their own problems, organizing themselves into regional groupings that co-operate on trade and security.

In a speech delivered at the Veterans of Foreign Wars

Convention in Ohio in the summer of 2004, President Bush declared that two major army divisions would be withdrawn from Germany, while a total of 60,000 to 70,000 troops would be deployed from Europe and Korea.[8] This is a recognition, after 9/11, that the biggest threats to US security and interests no longer come from Europe, but rather from the Middle East and Central Asia.

It is also a recognition of the fact that, at long last, Europeans are starting to take responsibility for their own security. In the 1990s, when the Balkans exploded, Europeans needed help from the Americans. But after the tense experience of depending on America in Bosnia and Kosovo, they have finally developed a capacity of their own – at least within their own continent. The biggest symbol of this new independence was the handover of control in Bosnia from NATO to the European Union in December 2004.

The same is increasingly true in other parts of the world. When East Timor collapsed, Australian troops, rather than American ones, were deployed to restore order on the troubled island. In Africa, a UN mission largely made up of Africans has been sent to the Congo, a South African-led mission has gone to Bujumbura in Burundi, and a UN mission to Sierra Leone (a third of which is African). American power is still vital in dealing with many global problems – from North Korea to Afghanistan. But, as the administration focuses ever more narrowly on threats to America's national security, other regions will increasingly have to take responsibility for their own affairs.

As we shall see in the next chapter, regional integration helps to equip countries and regions with more flexible means of tackling problems. But it also has implications for world order. As we move to a world of regions, America is in danger of falling behind. Its ideology of unilateralism has stopped it replicating the success of European enlargement in NAFTA, in spite of persistent demands from Mexico. Its military interventions in Haiti, Venezuela, or Colombia are different from the broad-based engagement one sees on the frontiers of the EU. And while popular revolutions in Georgia and Ukraine seek integration into Europe, the same movements in Venezuela and Bolivia, or new radical governments in Uruguay, Brazil and Argentina, seek greater autonomy from American hegemony.

Entering the Post-American World

American hegemony contains the seeds of its own destruction, and is already driving its own retreat.

The problem is that Washington's goals of defending itself while spreading democracy and human rights have become detached from a system that could deliver on them. During the Cold War they were embodied in international institutions like NATO and the United Nations, and American power was used to police them. But today, American power is pitched against the forces of globalization rather than moving in synchronicity with them. The war in Iraq was fought in the face of global public opinion, while the war on terror is conducted without the legitimating power of institutions that give allies a voice in deciding strategy. Military power can be a force for good, as it was in Bosnia, Kosovo, and Afghanistan. Assertive diplomacy can also be effective, as it has been with Libya since Lockerbie. But, without a system for regulating the exercise of power, American foreign policy will deliver a number of pyrrhic victories rather than a robust liberal democratic order.

Many Americans are already starting to question their lonely existence, and feeling the need for allies. The last few years have shown that America can inflict damage on the European project by splitting the continent into 'new' and 'old' parts, and by trying to thwart European initiatives like the International Criminal Court. But the country most damaged by anti-Europeanism is America itself. Its need for Europe has never been greater: in Afghanistan the mission is under French command; in Iran, it is Europeans who are leading the talks on WMD; in the Arab world, Europe is using its trade, investment, and diplomatic leverage to support democratization; and in Israel and Palestine, European money will pay for the measures that will make Sharon's withdrawal from Gaza possible.

In the longer term, as China and India become more powerful and start to play a more active role in the world, America will appreciate, once again, the need for international law and global institutions. Though it will continue to be the most powerful country in the world, its relative share of global power will decline, and it will not be able to use its military force to shape the behaviour of its peers.

The challenge for Europeans is to create a new system that embodies the transformative power of the rule of law and that reflects the three revolutions in global politics. The goal must not be to prevent America from defending itself, as many have suggested, but to place its actions in an institutional framework designed to tackle global challenges, rather than just national security. Europe needs a proactive

United States far more than an isolationist one. We will struggle to prevent global warming without working with the biggest polluter in the world; we will continue to rely on American military assistance even as we develop our defence identity; and we will be more likely to realize our own vision of a rule-governed world with American power behind it.

Because the European approach is more positive and peaceful, it is more likely to succeed in enlisting the rest of the world to solve global problems than George Bush's war on terror. And if it delivers real results, the Americans – like the cicadas in their capital city – will return from isolation and help Europe entrench a new world order.

CHAPTER 11

The Regional Domino Effect

Hugo Chavez is not the easiest of customers. The former army paratrooper, who attempted a coup in 1992, burst into Venezuelan electoral politics in 1998 when his 'Movement of the Fifth Republic' swept to power on the back of a promise to transform the lives of the poor, the dispossessed, and the weak. In his whirlwind term in office he has faced an attempted coup, general strikes, and a referendum; and he has not been afraid to make enemies. The populist leader of the world's fifth largest oil producer has attacked oil executives for living in 'luxury chalets where they perform orgies drinking whisky'; the Catholic Church for 'not walking in the path of Christ'; the media 'for being in the pay of reactionaries'; and the United States for 'fighting terror with terror'.[1] But there is one thing that this soldier turned politician does say yes to: Mercosur, the Common Market of the South.

Finally, after five protocols and a decade of applications

and failed attempts, Venezuela was admitted as an associate member on 8 July 2004, during a marathon meeting of the presidents (which also granted Mexico observer status, opening the way for it, too, to join in the future). This membership of Mercosur institutionalizes Venezuela's tight new economic and political relations with Argentina and Brazil (including a doubling of trade with the former, and a tripling with the latter). Chavez was jubilant: 'We want to see in our ships, in our pipes, in our medicines, and in other goods, the words "Made in Brazil" or "Made in Argentina" instead of "Made in the USA".'[2] Chavez's desire to join Mercosur is driven by more than the quixotic anti-Americanism that drove him to open friendly relations with Castro's Cuba and Saddam's Iraq. It comes from a recognition that the alliance is becoming critically important to the future of South America.

Regional integration took off in Latin America when the leaders of the big countries in the region saw the enormous advances being made in Europe with the creation of the Single European Market. The origins of the alliance come from an attempt to defuse the prickly relations between Brazil and Argentina, while – as recently as the 1970s – they were engaged in a nuclear arms race. But what started as a bilateral initiative between these two countries was broadened to include Paraguay and Uruguay in 1991 when Mercosur was formed (Chile and Bolivia joined as associate members in 1996). The member-states agreed to form a common market with co-ordinated macro-economic policies in different sectors, including foreign trade, agricultural, industrial, and fiscal. They also committed themselves to harmonize their legislation and create political and economic integration. Mercosur has a political structure that is loosely modelled on the European Union. The Common Market Council (CMG) is made up of foreign affairs ministers and ministers of economy. The chairmanship of the Council rotates every six months among member-states in alphabetical order.[3]

The early success was impressive. Tariffs were eliminated on most internal trade by 1995, and a common external tariff was agreed as well as a common customs code. The average tariff applied to third countries fell from 37.2 per cent in 1985 to a low of 11.5 per cent in 1994. As a result, intra-bloc trade boomed – rising from $4.1 billion in 1990 to $20.7 billion in 1997. What is more, foreign direct investment flooded in too: rising from $2 billion in 1991 to a peak of $56.6 billion in 1999.[4] Companies like Nestlé and Unilever reorganized their operations on a regional basis so that each product was made in a single factory for the region. In the car industry, firms such as Renault and Peugeot-Citroen, which had all but pulled out of the region, built new factories; Japanese companies also entered the regional market.

The creation of Mercosur had put the region on the world business map. But possibly the biggest success is the role that Mercosur has played in defending and strengthening democracy in South America's southern cone. After Brazil and Argentina helped to defuse an attempted coup in Paraguay in 1996, Mercosur formally included a 'democracy clause' as a condition for remaining in the group. The twenty-first century did not begin well for Mercosur, with financial turmoil in Brazil and Argentina; but the entry of Venezuela and Mexico, coupled with the improving position of the Brazilian and Argentine economies, have put the

Common Market back on track to eventually become an alliance that could integrate the whole of South America.[5]

Latin America is not alone. In Africa they have formed the African Union. Middle Eastern summits talk about the possibility of an Arab Union. East Asia has ASEAN and the Shanghai Co-operation Organization. South Asia has SAARC. The Pacific region has APEC. And North America has developed NAFTA and the Free Trade Area of the Americas to match the growing European single market.

While the global institutions such as the United Nations, the IMF and the World Bank continue to be playthings of the great powers, these regional organizations are starting to deliver real benefits. In Sudan in 2004, the African Union sent 4,000 troops to the Darfur region while the UN Security Council was bogged down in a debate about whether the violations really constituted genocide. In the Pacific, APEC is becoming a vehicle for promoting open trade and investment between the twenty-one countries of the region.[6] The Arab world is talking of turning the Arab League into an Arab Union – complete with parliament and single currency – to build on the progress that has already been made on an Arab Free Trade Agreement, the Arab Monetary Fund, and the Islamic Development Bank.

Together these developments spell the emergence of a world of regions. As they learn to work together, and experience real benefits, they will gradually start to pool sovereignty in the way that the European Union has pioneered.

The Regional Domino Effect

Many people have focused on the rise of great powers such as China and India and the implications they will have on world order. There is no doubt that they will challenge the 'unipolar world' shaped by the preferences of Americans and Europeans, who between them make up less than 10 per cent of the world's population. But an even bigger threat to the 'unipolar moment' comes from the fact that there is another tier of countries around the world – from Brazil and Mexico to South Africa and Nigeria, Japan and South Korea – that is no longer satisfied with dealing bilaterally with Europe and the United States and accepting the decisions that come from their relative position of weakness.

These countries have looked on at the way the European Union has given tiny countries an ability to shape their destiny on the world stage out of all proportion to their wealth, military might, or population size. They have seen that regional clubs can help to overcome historical rivalries and tensions, foster democracy, speed up the integration of countries into the world economy, and help to develop common solutions to problems that cut across borders – from organized crime to pollution. The EU's success has let the genie of regionalism out of the bottle, and it will be impossible to put it back in again. This new regionalism is not about autarchic blocs at war with one another: it is about clubs that promote global development, regional security, and open markets for their members. And as each region develops its own arrangements, they will cumulatively have an impact on world order.

Nearly five hundred years ago, Europe invented the most effective form of political organization in history: the nation-state. Through a series of wars and conquests, this form of political organization spread like a virus, so that by the twentieth century it was the only way of organizing politics – eliminating empires, city-states, and feudal systems. Because nation-states were most comfortable dealing with other nation-states, other political systems faced a stark choice: become a nation-state, or get taken over by one. By the end of the twentieth century the only way to have a seat at the table was to be a nation-state.

In the second half of the twentieth century, Europeans started to reinvent this model. As Europe develops ever greater global clout and spreads to take over a continent, other countries have been faced with an equally stark choice: join the European Union, or develop your own union based on the same principles of international law, interfering in each other's affairs, and peace as an ideology. By the end of the twenty-first century, in the new regional world, you will need to be part of a club to have a seat at the table. This is why countries are coming together to maintain their clout in the world. This 'regional domino effect' is already changing our ideas of politics and economics and redefining what power means for the twenty-first century.

The world that emerges will be centred around neither the United States nor the United Nations, but will be a community of interdependent regional clubs. In Africa, the focus on peace-keeping reflects the fact that conflict is the biggest enemy of development in the region – as well as the strong desire not to have to rely on Western troops to solve African problems. In East Asia, the 'Chiang Mai initiative' is an attempt to put in place an Asian solution to currency speculation so that in a future Asian currency crisis member countries will not be forced to turn to the International Monetary Fund. Although under present rules the initiative will only lend members 10 per cent of their short-term financial assistance (with the remaining 90 per cent depending on IMF criteria), in the medium term it is likely that this region, which is famously awash with capital, will change the criteria to free itself from the IMF and the World Bank. In Latin America, too, economists have calculated that there are enough reserves in the continent to deal with any crisis (short of a meltdown of the Brazilian economy) without recourse to the IMF.[7]

The uniting factor behind all these initiatives is an attempt to get beyond the 'unipolar world'. No country wants to be dictated to by superpowers or global institutions that they cannot control. In this world, it will be possible to maintain your identity and your sovereignty without being a superpower. But it will also be impossible to commit mass human rights abuses or genocide and use the United Nations' doctrine of 'non-interference in internal affairs'[8] as a geopolitical do-not-disturb sign.

Europe's Role in Promoting this New World Order

If regional organizations did not exist, they would need to be invented. Their rise is inexorable and startlingly rapid. But although this world is emerging of its own accord, Europe can give it a helping hand. The Americans precipitated the creation of the European Union by insisting that European countries had to work together if they wanted to get access to the money made available under the Marshall Plan after the Second World War. They made it a political reality by developing mutual security arrangements through NATO rather than dealing with each country individually.

The European Union could do the same thing. As the biggest donor in the world, Europe could use its aid to promote intra-regional co-operation, tying money to economic integration, regional infrastructure projects, and regional organizations' contribution to security. The EU has made a move in this direction through its 2003 approval for the African Peace Facility, which will provide 'financial muscle' for peace-keeping missions led by the African Union.[9] It should use its position as the biggest market in the world to tie progress in world trade talks to the removal of regional trade barriers. And it should use its growing political voice to upgrade the importance of region-to-region dialogue. Instead of hatching deals with China, South Africa, and Brazil, we should aim to make important decisions in EU–Mercosur, ASEM, and EU–AU summits.

In the long term, Europe's goal should be to create a Union of Unions that brings these regional organizations together, in the way that the European Union brought the Coal and Steel Community, Euratom, and the European Community together into a single European Economic Community. A 'Community of Regional Entities' could become the primary co-ordinating body of the United Nations. This would not necessarily have to replace the Security Council and General Assembly, but the forum for regional organizations would be the best place to deal with the two most pressing issues on the global agenda: development and peace-keeping. [10]

Our experience with the European Union has shown that the way to construct a new order will not be to start with a grand constitutional design but to create an interest in working together on the pressing problems. By forming a series of overlapping clubs to deal with trade, nuclear proliferation, economic development, global diseases, and propping up failing states, it might one day be possible to bring them together into a single framework.[11]

As the momentum for regional organization picks up, great powers like the United States will inevitably be sucked into the process of integration. They might be able to slow the process, but they won't be able to stop it. By opposing it they will harm themselves by provoking regional clubs to organise against them. However if they embrace it, they will enhance their power, and by doing so act as midwives for this emerging new world order. As this process continues, we will see the emergence of a 'New European Century'. Not because Europe will run the world as an empire, but because the European way of doing things will have become the world's.

APPENDIX

The 109 Countries of the Eurosphere

The Eurosphere includes the 25 existing members of the European Union, three countries which have applied for membership (Turkey, Romania and Bulgaria), and the 81 countries listed below.

Western Balkans (5)
Albania
Bosnia and Herzegovina
Croatia
FYR Macedonia
FR Yugoslavia

European CIS (8)
Armenia
Azerbaijan
Belarus
Georgia
Kazakhstan
Moldova

Russia
Ukraine

Middle East and Northern Africa (19)
Algeria
Bahrain
Egypt
Iran
Iraq
Israel
Jordan
Kuwait
Lebanon

Libya
Morocco
Oman
Palestinian Territories
Qatar
Saudi Arabia
Syria
Tunisia
United Arab Emirates
Yemen

Sub-Saharan Africa (49)
Angola
Benin
Botswana
Burkina Faso
Burundi
Cameroon
Cape Verde
Central African Rep
Chad
Comoros
Congo, Dem Rep
Congo, Rep
Côte d'Ivoire
Djibouti
Equatorial Guinea
Eritrea
Ethiopia
Gabon
Gambia

Ghana
Guinea
Guinea-Bissau
Kenya
Lesotho
Liberia
Madagascar
Malawi
Mali
Mauritania
Mauritius
Mayotte
Mozambique
Namibia
Niger
Nigeria
Rwanda
São Tomé & Principe
Senegal
Seychelles
Sierra Leone
Somalia
South Africa
Sudan
Swaziland
Tanzania
Togo
Uganda
Zambia
Zimbabwe

NOTES

Introduction

1 Emmott, Bill (2003), *Vision 20/21*, London: Penguin.

2 Fukuyama, Francis (Winter 1990–1), 'The Unipolar Moment', *Foreign Affairs*.

3 Joseph Nye has written a number of works on 'soft' and 'hard' power, some of which include *Soft Power: The Means to Success in World Politics* (2004), *The Paradox of American Power: Why the World's Only Superpower Can't Go It Alone* (2003), and *Bound to Lead: The Changing Nature of American Power* (1990).

4 Calleo, David (Summer 2003), 'Power and Deficit Spending', *The National Interest*.

5 Ibid.

6 A fascinating paper published by the European Central Bank called 'Economic Relations with Regions Neighbouring the Euro Area in the "Euro Time Zone"' (December 2002) by Francesco Mazzafero, Arnaud Mehl, Michael Sturm, Christian Thimann, and Adalbert Winkler calls these countries the 'euro time zone' and examines the economic, monetary, and financial relations between them and the European Union.

7 I am grateful to my colleague Richard Youngs, who in his

work *Sharpening European Engagement* (2004), published by the Foreign Policy Centre, employs the phrase 'transformative power' when characterizing the nature of Europe.

8 Rifkin, Jeremy (2004), *European Dream*, London: Jeremy P. Tarcher/Penguin.

Chapter 1

1 Mazower, Mark (1999), *Dark Continent: Europe's Twentieth Century*, London: Penguin.

2 Valéry, Paul (1921), Essay entitled *'On European Civilization and the European Mind'* (1919, 1922)

3 Schuman, Robert (9 May 1950), *Schuman Declaration.* For additional analysis see Dick Leonard and Mark Leonard's *Pro-European Reader* (2002), London: Palgrave Macmillan.

4 Duchêne, François (1994), *Jean Monnet: The First Statesman of Interdependence*, New York and London: Norton.

5 Ibid.

6 Ibid.

7 Smith, Adam (1776), *An Inquiry into the Nature and Causes of the Wealth of Nations.*

8 I am grateful to Ana Palacio for suggesting this evocative metaphor to me.

9 Miller, Vaughne (2004), *EC Legislation*, Standard Note SN/IA/2888, London: House of Commons Library.

10 Nugent, Neill (2003, 5th edn), *The Government and Politics of the European Union*, Basingstoke: Palgrave Macmillan.

11 DTI (1994) *Review of the implementation and enforcement of EC law in the UK*, 1994 Efficiency Scrutiny Report, DTI, London. The amount varies widely from Department to Department. According the House of Commons Library, in the 2003–4 Parliamentary Session it ranged from 1 per cent in the DFES, 10 per cent in the Department for Work and Pensions, 20 per cent in the Home Office, 25 per cent in the DTI to 50 per cent in DEFRA.

12 Nugent 2003, op. cit.

13 Brussels Capital Region Website.

14 John Hume's acceptance speech (10 December 1998) can be

accessed at http://cain.ulst.ac.uk/events/peace/docs/nobeljh.htm.
15 Duchêne (1994) op. cit.

Chapter 2

1 These statistics were accessed from
   www.corporate.visa.com/corporate.JSP
2 Mitchell Waldrop, M. (October/November 1996), 'The
   Trillion-Dollar Vision of Dee Hock', *Fast Company*, p. 75.
3 Manuel Castells was the first to make this point in the third
   volume of his visionary *Information Society* trilogy, *The End
   of Millennium*.
4 Westlake, Martin (1999), *The Council of the European Union*,
   London: John Harper Publishing.
5 Nugent 2003, op. cit.
6 Ibid.
7 The best introduction to the European Union is Dick
   Leonard's *The Economist Guide to the European Union*
   (2004), 9th edition (London: Profile).
8 Dr Henry Kissinger famously coined this phrase.
9 Bobbit, Philip (2003), *The Shield of Achilles: War, Peace and
   the Course of History*, London: Penguin.
10 Ibid.
11 This argument is discussed further in Paul Kennedy's *The Rise
   and Fall of the Great Powers*, 1988 (London: Fontana).
12 *The Postmodern State and the World Order* (Demos/The
   Foreign Policy Centre, 2000) is available from
   www.fpc.org.uk.
13 Rosecrance, Richard (1998), 'The European Union: A New
   Type of International Actor', in *Paradoxes of European
   Foreign Policy*, ed. Jan Zielonka, Kluwer.
14 Mead, Walter Russell (March/April 2004), 'America's Sticky
   Power', *Foreign Policy*.
15 Peel, Quentin (12 March 2003), *Financial Times*, 'Europe is
   first casualty of war'.
16 Robert Kagan's argument can be explored further in his book,
   *Of Paradise and Power: America and Europe in the New
   World Order* 2004 (New York: Random House).

Chapter 3

1 Ullman, Harlan K., and James P. Wade(1996), *Shock and Awe: Achieving Rapid Dominance*, NDU Press Book, December.
2 Jessica Mathews (Aug 2002) 'A New Approach: Coercive Inspections', *Iraq, A New Approach* Carnegie Endowment for International Peace.
3 Excerpt from 'Panopticism' in Foucault, Michel (1995), *Discipline and Punish: The Birth of the Prison*, New York: Vintage Books), pp. 195–228, tr. from the French by Alan Sheridan (translation © 1977).
4 Duchêne, François (1904), *Jean Monnet: The First Statesman of Independence* (New York and London: Norton).
5 Mearsheimer, John, *Back to the Future*, International Security, 15:1 (Summer 1990).
6 US Department of state (18 June 2002) 'Conventional Armed Forces in Europe (CFE Treaty)', Fact Sheet, Bureau of Arms Control, Washington DC.
7 Robert Cooper makes this point effectively in *The Breaking of Nations*, 2004 (London: Atlantic Books).
8 Leonard, Dick (2004) The Economist Guide to the European Union, 9th edition (London: Profile)
9 Office of Public Communications, State House Abuja (Feb 2004) President Obasanjo Chairs NEPAD Peer Review Forum.
10 Max Weber famously defined the state as 'a human community that (successfully) claims the monopoly of the legitimate use of physical force within a given territory', originally delivered from a speech entitled 'Politics as a Vocation' in 1998 at Munich University.

Chapter 4

1 See 'Will Turkey Make It?' by Stephen Kinzer, *New York Review of Books* (15 July 2004), and Amanda Ackcakoca, 'Turkey's accession to the EU: Time for a leap of faith', Commentary, European Policy Centre (23 June 2004).
2 In doing this it acts in much the same way as the sociologist Ulrich Beck describes the global capitalist system acting, and much of what Beck has to say about the radical and

transformative effect of the kind of power that global capital wields applies *mutatis mutandis* to European power. In a lecture at the London School of Economics, Beck described the dynamics of power in a globalized economy. He argued that the world economy now wields what he termed a 'meta power', a power that is able to change the very nature of power in international affairs. The new power of the global economy is based on threat of withdrawal, in just the same way that European influence is.

3 Blum, William (1995), *Killing Hope: US Military and CIA Interventionism Since World War II*, Monroe, Maine: Common Courage Press. Updated list provided by Zoltan Grossman, 'A Century of US Military Interventions: From Wounded Knee to Haiti', 2004 (www.uwec.edu/grossmzc/peace.html).

4 Centre for Information Policy (February 2003), 'U.S. Support for Plan Colombia' (www.ciponline.org/facts/coaid.htm).

5 US Department of State (14 March 2001), 'Plan Colombia', Fact Sheet, Bureau of Western Hemisphere Affairs, Washington, DC.

6 La Fontaine, 'Le Laboureur et ses enfants'.

7 'Economic Relations with Regions Neighbouring the Euro Area in the "Euro Time Zone"' (December 2002) by Francesco Mazzafero, Arnaud Mehl, Michael Sturm, Christian Thimann, and Adalbert Winkler.

8 The EU has signed the Stabilization and Association Agreements with the Western Balkans; the Partnership and Co-operation Agreements with Russia and Commonwealth of Independent States; the Mediterranean Agreements with countries around the Mediterranean; and the Yaoundé-Lomé-Cotonou agreements with African countries.

9 Rosencrance 1998, op. cit.

Chapter 5

1 This title is drawn from an interesting collection of essays published by the Centre for European Reform in 2004. Everts, et al (2004) European Way of War, Centre for European Reform, London.

2 BBC News (20 February 2003), 'Srebrenica timeline' (http://news.bbc.co.uk/1/hi/world/europe/675945.stm).

3 Simms, Brendan (2002), *Unfinest Hour: Britain and the Destruction of Bosnia*, London: Penguin.

4 Howard, Michael (2002), *The Invention of Peace and Reinvention of War*, London: Profile Books.

5 Von Clausewitz, Karl (1984), *On War*, ed. and tr. by Michael Howard and Peter Paret, with commentary by Bernard Brodie, Princeton: Princeton University Press.

6 This was echoed by speeches of other prominent European politicians such as Joshka Fischer in Germany, who said in his speech on transatlantic relations (27 June 2002): 'Security, as we perceive it, concerns society as a whole, concerns also the ecological, economic, social and cultural aspects of the way societies evolve. That is the approach we have taken in the Balkans and that is what we are now trying to do in Afghanistan. These are the things we Europeans must rigorously push for at the international level as the 21st century unfolds.'

7 Giegerich, Bastian, and William Wallace (2004), 'Not Such a Soft Power: The External Deployment of European Forces', *Survival*, 46, pp. 163–82.

8 Gourlay, Catriona (19 October 2003), 'Operations update: Past, Present and Future', ISIS Europe, European Security Review.

9 This phrase comes from former Swedish Prime Minister Carl Bildt's speech to the Ivan Bloch Commemorative Conference on the Future of War, St Petersburg, Russia (25 February 1999).

10 These figures come from a speech given by UK Foreign Secretary Jack Straw entitled 'Failed and Failing States' at the European Research Institute, University of Birmingham (6 September 2002).

11 Carl Bildt made this point well in his *Financial Times* article 'We must build states and not nations' (16 January 2004).

12 Everts, Steven et al. (2004), *European Way of War*, London, Centre for European Reform.

13 Everts et al., (2004).

14 Ibid.

15 Lieven, Anatol, (April 2001), 'Soldiers Before Missiles: Meeting the Challenge from the World's Streets', *Carnegie Endowment for International Peace*, vol.1, no. 4.

16 Freedman in Everts et al. 2004.

17 O'Hanlon in Everts et al. 2004.

18 Ibid.

19 These commitments were made at the Helsinki and Gothenburg Summits. Sources for the figures include Moravcsik, Andrew (3 April 2003), 'How Europe can win without an army', *Financial Times*; and Everts et al. 2004.

Chapter 6

1 I remember the late Swedish Foreign Minister, Anna Lindh, telling me how she used to hide her Mickey Mouse in hardback books – like pornography – so that her parents wouldn't catch her entertaining herself with capitalist mascots. But they also act as a metaphor for perceptions of the European economy.

2 Storrie, Donald 'The Regulation and Growth of Contingent Employment in Sweden.' CELMS, Goteborg University

3 Charles Leadbeater has argued convincingly that there is a 'Helsinki spirit' in his yet to be published articles 'Adaptive Social Democracy' and 'The Helsinki Spirit.'

4 Murray, Alasdair (March 2004) *The Lisbon Scorecard IV*, Centre for European Reform.

5 A series of 'revisionist' accounts of the economics of the 1990s make this point well. Most notable are Hutton, Will (2002) *The World We're In*, London, Little Brown; Blanchard, Olivier (September 2003), 'European growth over the coming decade'; Kay, John (2004) 'Economic Reform in Europe – Priorities for the next five years', Edited by Roger Liddle and Maria João Rodrigues, Policy Network, London; Legrain Phillippe (16 June 2003) 'Europe's Mighty Economy', *New Republic*; and Daly, Kevin (26 June 2004) 'Euro-zone economy holding its own compared to achievements in the US', *Irish Times*.

6 *Wall Street Journal* (27 August 2004), Sarah Lueck and John D. McKinnon, 'Ranks of the poor, uninsured grew last year in the US.'

7 *The Economist* (19 June 2004) 'Mirror, mirror on the wall – Europe v. America'.

8 *The Economist* (19 June 2004) 'Mirror, mirror on the wall – Europe v. America'.

9 Kevin Daly uses a whole economy measure of productivity. The commonly quoted US non-farm, business productivity data suggests faster growth because, once one strips out two large sectors – farming and the government – where productivity growth is low, productivity growth in the remainder of economy seems quite high.

10 Adair Turner made this apparent in a lecture he gave at the London School of Economics entitled 'What's wrong with the European economy' on 10 February 2003.

11 This was made clear in a report entitled 'How Does the United States Compare' in the OECD Employment Outlook 2004.

12 My colleague Keith Didcock includes these figures in his paper entitled 'Can Europe Sharpen its Blunt Competitive edge?' given at the Prague Castle Conference 2004.

13 Rifkin, Jeremy, (2004), *The European Dream*, Penguin/Tarcher, New York.

14 Murray, Alasdair (March 2004) *The Lisbon Scorecard IV*, Centre for European Reform.

15 Rifkin (2004)

16 Rifkin (2004)

17 *The Economist*, (Mar 13th 2003), 'Revitalising Old Europe'.

18 The problem is that, in the past, many governments have used early retirement schemes as a means of deflating the unemployment figures. When companies need to cut costs they will also often offer the oldest workers a chance to retire early. As a result, the real average age of retirement for EU male workers is 60, compared with the statutory average of 65 (in Greece only one in five actually works to 65).

19 Joint report by the Commission and the Council on adequate and sustainable pensions, as approved by the Council

(EPSCO/Ecofin) on 6/7 March 2003.

20 Mazaferro et al. (2004). It is true that together these countries only make up 4 per cent of world GDP and tend to be those geographically linked to the Euro (like the Western Balkans, Montenegro and Kosovo), or part of the CFA franc zone, but the percentage is growing.

21 *Environmental Protection, Environmental Energy and Technology* (2004), Stockholm, Swedish Institute.

22 The US government's International Energy Outlook 2003, Energy Information Administration of the Department of Energy (www.eia.doe.gov).

23 European Commission (2003), *The Internal Market: Ten Years Without Frontiers*, Brussels.

24 'The Economic Impact of Enlargement', a Study by the Directorate General for Economic and Financial Affairs, May 2001.

25 They leave out Canada as it accounts for only 3 per cent of the G7's GDP.

26 China is tipped to overtake Germany by 2007, Japan by 2015, and America by 2041. India could overtake Japan by 2032. All four BRICs will be bigger than any Western European economy by 2036. Of today's G6, only America and Japan would then still be among the world's six biggest economies.

27 *Building The New Europe* published by Lehman Brothers, authors Michael Hume, John Dew and Silja Sepping, 28 April 2004.

28 Gordon, Robert, (June 2004), 'Two Centuries of Economic Growth: Europe Chasing the American Frontier', Discussion Paper No. 4415, London, Centre for Economic Policy Research.

Chapter 7

1 Milward, Alan S. (1994), *European Rescue of the Nation State*, London: Routledge.

2 For an extremely compelling and contrasting analysis of EU legitimacy see Simon Hix's *The Political System of the European Union (1999)* Palgrave Macmillan.

3 Moravcsik, Andrew (2002), 'In Defense of the "Democratic Deficit": Reassessing Legitimacy in the European Union', *Journal of Common Market Studies*, vol. 40, no. 4, p. 607.

4 Ibid.

5 Hix, Simon.

6 Gould, Philip (2003), 'The Empty Stadium', *Progressive Politics*, vol. 2.3.

7 Bevanger, Lars (1 May 2003), 'Norway's EU debate re-surfaces', BBC News (http://news.bbc.co.uk/1/hi/world/europe/2991833.stm).

8 The debate in Norway about EU membership is increasingly polarized, with many calling on Norway to join the EU and some arguing that it should leave the EEA, as no one thinks the status quo is tenable for much longer. The only reason Norway remains outside the EU is because it subsidizes its agriculture at a higher level than would be allowed under the CAP and can only afford to do this because of North Sea oil and gas. Hence, Norwegian farmers are very anti-European. But this is a luxury only a few states can afford, and is hence *not* a model for the UK.

9 House of Commons Hansard Debates (20 November 1991).

10 Alan Milward's book *European Rescue of the Nation State* explains this well.

11 My former colleague Tom Arbuthnott explores this point in more depth in his intriguing pamphlet, *Can Europe Save National Democracy*, London: The Foreign Policy Centre, 2003.

12 I have written about ways of inputting European democracy in *European Democracy: A Manifesto* and *Network Europe* published by the Foreign Policy Centre (2004).

13 Norman, Peter (2003), *The Accidental Constitution*, Brussels: EuroComment.

14 Ibid.

15 Moravcsik, Andrew (2002), 'In Defense of the "Democratic Deficit": Reassessing Legitimacy in the European Union', *Journal of Common Market Studies*, vol. 40, no. 4, p. 607.

Chapter 8

1 De Tocqueville, Alexis (1837) *letter from Algeria*, 22 August.

2 Heather Grabbe estimates that the EU spent 67 billion Euros on enlargement between 2000–2004, compared to $200 billion on Iraq. 'Profiting from EU enlargement' (June 2001) CER

3 BBC News (25 January 2004) 'Georgia swears in new president' (http://news.bbc.co.uk/1/hi/world/europe/3426977.stm).

4 World Economic Forum (29 April 2004), 'European Economic Summit 2004' (http://www.weforum.org/site/knowledgenavigator.nsf).

5 The Middle East Media Research Institute (24 December 2003), 'Arab Columnists Envy Georgia's Political Revolution: Tbilisi Spring, Arab Winter'.

6 Ibid.

7 The Middle East Media Research Institute (6 January 2003), 'Arab Media Reactions to the US–Middle East Partnership Initiative Part I: Opponents' Views'.

8 Mortimer, Edward, and Francis Ghiles(28 October 1994), 'The discreet intermediary', *Financial Times*.

9 Jan Zielonka argues that 'globalisation and interdependence may render prohibitive the costs of controlling the flow of goods, capital, services and people across borders ... and the "fortress" impulse undermines the coherence, moral authority, and international credibility of the EU'. In Zielonka, Jan (2002) Europe Unbound: Enlarging and Reshaping the Boundaries of European Union (London: Routledge).

10 Wallace 2003.

11 Ibid.

12 O'Rourke, Breffni (31 January 2003), 'Prodi sets out vision of 'Ring of Friends', closer ties with neighbours' (http://www.eubusiness.com/imported/2003/01/102393/).

13 In March 2003 the European Commission published a remarkable document that was aimed to turn this vision into a reality: *Wider Europe – Neighbourhood: A New Framework for Relations With Our Eastern and Southern Neighbours.*

14 Youngs, Richard (2004), 'European Policies for Middle East Reform: A Ten Point Action Plan', London: Foreign Policy

Centre.

15 Ron Asmus and Ken Pollack make this point in a very prescient article in *Policy Review*

16 Johnson, Chalmers (19 January 2004), 'The Arithmetic of America's Military Bases Abroad: What Does It All Add Up To?', History News Network (http://hnn.us/articles/3097.html).

Chapter 9

1 *CIA World Factbook* (2004) (http://www.cia.gov/cia/publications/factbook/geos/ch.html#Econ).

2 Ramo, Joshua (2004), *The Beijing Consensus*, London: The Foreign Policy Centre. This is a brilliant introduction to new thinking in China which shows that the impact of the country's success and ideas is already outstripping China's economic and military power.

3 An, Qing (22 April 2004), 'China Peaceful Rising Spin Doctor's Antidote to China Threat', BOAO Forum for Asia (http://en.chinabroadcast.cn/1325/2004-4-23/20@106774.htm).

4 Former Chinese President Jiang Zemin spoke extensively about the need for China's 'rejuvenation' in a speech in Cambridge on 22 October 1999.

5 *China Daily* (8 November 2002), 'Jury out on effect of WTO' (http://www.chinadaily.com.cn/chinagate/doc/2002-11/08/content_249310.htm).

6 Ching, Frank (27 February 2004), 'China's actions must match its words', *Business Times*, Singapore.

7 Xuetong, Yan, 'Foreign policy for regional stability', *Beijing Review*.

8 See Evan S. Medeiros's article 'China Debates its "Peaceful Rise" Strategy' in *YaleGlobal* (22 June 2004) for a brief reflection on the change of the term 'Peaceful Rise'.

9 Robert W. Radtke, 'China's "Peaceful Rise" overshadowing US influence in Asia?', *Christian Science Monitor* (8 December 2003).

10 *Encarta*, 'China' (http://encarta.msn.com/encyclopedia_761573055_11/China.html#endads).

11 Ramo 2004, op, cit.

12 He was speaking at the sixth ASEM Foreign Minister's Meeting in County Kildare in 2004.

13 Oresman, Matthew (1 May 2004), 'Catching the Shanghai Spirit', *Foreign Policy*, no. 142, p. 78.

14 Sneider, Daniel (23 March 2004), 'China's stunning ascent', *San Jose Mercury News*.

15 Wang Jisi (which article?).

16 Clinton, Bill (19 December 2002), 'Bill Clinton: America should lead, not dominate', Tribune Media Services International (http://www.iht.com/articles/80709.html).

Chapter 10

1 Aron, Raymond (1974), *The Imperial Republic: The United States and the World 1945–1973*, New Jersey: Prentice Hall.

2 Garton Ash, Timothy (2004) *Free World: Why a Crisis of the West Reveals the Opportunity of Our Time* (Penguin, Allen Lane).

3 *China Business Weekly* (5 August 2004), 'China to diversify foreign exchange reserves'.

4 Reuters (13 November 2004), 'Indian foreign currency reserves at record $122 bln'.

5 See Usborne, David (15 December 1996), 'Dire States: Americans are used to resentment of their global dominance', *The Independent*.

6 See Daalder, Ivo, and Lindsay, James (23 May 2004), 'An Alliance of Democracies', *The Washington Post*.

7 The philanthropist and human rights campaigner, George Soros, has been leading a movement to turn the 'Community of Democracies' into an effective caucus in the United Nations – to establish a principle that democracies will be treated differently (and better) than non-democracies in the international system. One of his staff, Thomas Palley, has produced an interesting paper arguing that membership of the Community of Democracies would be a criterion that countries need to meet in order to benefit from the US Government's Millennium Challenge Account.

8 BBC News (17 August 2004), 'Shake-up for US troops over-

seas' (http://news.bbc.co.uk/1/hi/world/americas/3568548.stm).

Chapter 11

1 BBC News (16 March 2004), 'Profile: Hugo Chavez' (http://news.bbc.co.uk/1/hi/world/americas/3517106.stm).
2 Guerrero, Modesto Emilio (9 July 2004), 'Venezuela's Triumph in Mercosur', Venezuelanalysis.com.
3 Reid, Michael (2002), 'Mercosur: a critical overview', Chatham House.
4 Ibid.
5 Ibid.
6 Dervis, Kemal, 'Better globalisation perspective on legitimacy reform and global governance', Ceren Ozer, Centre for Global Development.
7 I am grateful to Stephanie Griffith Jones for drawing this to my attention.
8 Article Five of the UN Charter.
9 I am grateful to my colleague Richard Gowan, who spells this out in this article 'The EU, Regional Organisations and Security: Strategic Partners or Convenient Alibis?, *Egmont Paper No. 3: Audit of European Strategy*, Royal Institute for International Relations, Brussels (2004).
10 I analyse these issues in greater detail in 'Global Europe: Implementing the European Security Strategy' (2004), written with my colleague Richard Gowan.
11 Slaughter, Ann-Marie (2004), *A New World Order*, New Jersey: Princeton University Press.

ACKNOWLEDGEMENTS

Europe's enemies might never forgive it the banality of its success. But I would like to celebrate it, to tell the tale of Europe's escape from history, and to see how the lessons of that journey could help shape a more peaceful twenty-first century. My generation is the first in four generations of my family not to face war, persecution, exile, or even extermination. This book is an extended thank you letter to the visionaries on both sides of the Atlantic who have managed to create a Europe without drama.

There are many people who have made it possible for the book to happen.

First, the support of two unique institutions. The German Marshall Fund of the United States, under the leadership of its indefatigable and visionary President Craig Kennedy, was kind enough to think the project worth supporting, giving me a 'Transatlantic Fellowship', providing me with a home in Washington DC for five months, and opening the door to a remarkable community of thinkers and do-ers on both sides of the Atlantic. During my time in Washington, the staff of the

GMF were like a surrogate family feeding me ideas, contacts, and inspiring me through their prodigious ability to get things done. I would like to thank Ronald Asmus, John Audley, Jeff Bergner, Maia Comeau, Mark Cunningham, Abigail Golden-Vazquez, Patricia Griffin, Nicola Hagen, Phillip Henderson, Myles Nienstadt, Ellen Pope, Sara Reckless, Kareem Saleh, Jeremiah Schatt, Susan Sechler, Ursula Soyez, Dan Twining, and Claudia Chantal Zackariya.

I must also thank the Board, Advisory Council and staff of the Foreign Policy Centre for allowing me to experience the pride and joy of creating and running the FPC for six happy years, and then continuing to give me support to work on this project, even while I was in America. I am grateful to Michael Levy, Liz Lloyd, Adam Lury, Fred Halliday, Meta Ramsay, Michael Butler, Stephen Twigg, Miles Webber, and above all Andrew Hood. I always value the intellectual companionship I have had from all my staff including Lucy Ahad, Greg Austin, Rob Blackhurst, Keith Didcock, Richard Gowan, Phoebe Griffith, Rouzbeh Pirouz, Andrew Small, and Mark Spokes.

A series of stellar research assistants supplied both intellectual and organisational support in London and Washington: Conrad Smewing, without whose penetrating intelligence and dedication this book would never have even been started; Julian von Fummetti whose stalwart assistance was crucial during my sabbatical in Washington DC; Richard Tite who provided material and insights for the chapter on economics; and Nadia Shabbaz who was with me at the end of the project, checking facts, and casting her eagle eye over numerous drafts.

I have presented some of the thoughts that turned into chapters at seminars where I have got invaluable feedback. At the British Council's Prague Castle conference in 2003, the positive reactions of people like Christopher Coker, A.C. Grayling, Hamish McCrae, Sacha Vondra, and Michael

Zantovsky all encouraged me to write a book. In February 2004, I spoke at a seminar at the LSE organised by George Lawson, where he along with Barry Buzan, Michael Cox, Chris Hill, and William Wallace gave me advice which has stood me in good stead. In Washington, the German Marshall Fund organised a lunch time seminar where I got friendly criticism and many ideas on how to strengthen my case for an American audience. Later at a GMF Conference in Dublin I was able to strengthen my arguments further after I shared a panel with the incomparable Walter Russell Mead. The British Council and the European Commission funded a conference in June on 'Global Europe' at Wilton Park where my ideas were tested by participants from most of the EU member states, the US, and Asia. Finally, I was invited to give a lecture at St Antony's College Oxford, organised by Jan Zielonka and Timothy Garton Ash, two of the most creative and compelling thinkers on the future of Europe.

I have also benefited from talking through my thesis with many of the thinkers I admire the most. They include Phillip Bobbitt, Robert Cooper, Ivo Daalder, Daniel Drezner, Espen Barth Eide, Anthony Giddens, Ulrike Guérot, Fiona Hill, Stanley Hoffman, Rem Koolhaas, Stephen Krasner, Ian Lesser, Anatol Lieven, James Lindsay, Jessica Mathews, Mike McFaul, John Mearsheimer, Andrew Moravcsik, Geoff Mulgan, Joseph Nye, Martin Ortega, Ana Palacio, Bary Posen, Richard Rosecrance, Joshua Ramo, Michael Von der Schulenberg, Jeremy Shapiro, Radek Sikorski, Jim Steinberg, and Fareed Zakaria.

Malcolm Chalmers, Richard Gowan, Charles Grant, Simon Hix, Michael Hume, Philippe Legrain, Alasdair Murray, Andrew Small, Peter Wilson, Richard Youngs, Joshua Ramo all read some or all of the book in draft form and have improved them immeasurably through their comments.

While I was planning and writing the book, I was watched

over by three intellectual godfathers. Michael Butler, one of the creators of today's European Union through his hard labours in Brussels, has given me rock-solid support on this project, as on so many others since I got to know him through the Foreign Policy Centre. Geoffrey Edwards, who taught me how the European Union, which I'd experienced in practice, works in theory has ploughed through various drafts and been ever available to talk through ideas. Bill Antholis was the perfect sounding-board, foil and dinner-host in Washington. Without his encouragement this book would never have been written.

My agent Maggie Pearlstine, and her colleague Jamie Crawford, immediately embraced the idea, helped to conceive of it as a book, and found a first-rate publisher, Fourth Estate, which has turned out to be a wonderful home for it. Caroline Michel and Nicholas Pearson instinctively understood the point of the book, Natasa Kennedy and Andrea Joyce have done a phenomenal job selling the rights to publishers across Europe, Robin Harvie has shown a remarkable commitment and ability to make my ideas spread to where books about Europe usually fail to reach. But, above all I must thank my editor, Mitzi Angel, for her wisdom, patience, and dedication. She is everything one could hope for in an editor and more.

Finally, I must thank my family to whom this volume is dedicated. My fiancée Gabrielle, my mother Irène, my father Dick, and my sister Miriam are the dancing stars of my galaxy. Their love, generosity, and tender criticism make life a gift.

INDEX

PUBLICAFFAIRS is a publishing house founded in 1997. It is a tribute to the standards, values, and flair of three persons who have served as mentors to countless reporters, writers, editors, and book people of all kinds, including me.

I. F. STONE, proprietor of *I. F. Stone's Weekly,* combined a commitment to the First Amendment with entrepreneurial zeal and reporting skill and became one of the great independent journalists in American history. At the age of eighty, Izzy published *The Trial of Socrates,* which was a national bestseller. He wrote the book after he taught himself ancient Greek.

BENJAMIN C. BRADLEE was for nearly thirty years the charismatic editorial leader of *The Washington Post.* It was Ben who gave the *Post* the range and courage to pursue such historic issues as Watergate. He supported his reporters with a tenacity that made them fearless, and it is no accident that so many became authors of influential, best-selling books.

ROBERT L. BERNSTEIN, the chief executive of Random House for more than a quarter century, guided one of the nation's premier publishing houses. Bob was personally responsible for many books of political dissent and argument that challenged tyranny around the globe. He is also the founder and was the longtime chair of Human Rights Watch, one of the most respected human rights organizations in the world.

.   .   .

For fifty years, the banner of Public Affairs Press was carried by its owner Morris B. Schnapper, who published Gandhi, Nasser, Toynbee, Truman, and about 1,500 other authors. In 1983 Schnapper was described by *The Washington Post* as "a redoubtable gadfly." His legacy will endure in the books to come.

Peter Osnos, *Publisher*